BUILDING
HISTORY
SERIES

THE
VATICAN

Titles in the Building History Series Include:

Alcatraz
The Atom Bomb
The Canals of Venice
The Eiffel Tower
The Golden Gate Bridge
The Great Wall of China
The Holy City of Jerusalem
The Hoover Dam
Machu Picchu
The Medieval Castle
The Medieval Cathedral
Mount Rushmore
The New York Subway System
The Palace of Versailles
The Panama Canal
The Parthenon of Ancient Greece
The Pyramids of Giza
The Roman Colosseum
Roman Roads and Aqueducts
The Russian Kremlin
Shakespeare's Globe
The Sistine Chapel
The Space Shuttle
The Statue of Liberty
Stonehenge
The Suez Canal
The Taj Mahal
The Titanic
The Tower of Pisa
The Transcontinental Railroad
The Viking Longship
The White House
The World Trade Center

BUILDING HISTORY SERIES

THE VATICAN

by William W. Lace

LUCENT BOOKS®

San Diego • Detroit • New York • San Francisco • Cleveland
New Haven, Conn. • Waterville, Maine • London • Munich

© 2004 by Lucent Books. Lucent Books is an imprint of The Gale Group, Inc.,
a division of Thomson Learning, Inc.

Lucent Books® and Thomson Learning™ are trademarks used herein under license.

For more information, contact
Lucent Books
27500 Drake Rd.
Farmington Hills, MI 48331-3535
Or you can visit our Internet site at http://www.gale.com

ALL RIGHTS RESERVED.
No part of this work covered by the copyright hereon may be reproduced or used in any form or by any means—graphic, electronic, or mechanical, including photocopying, recording, taping, Web distribution or information storage retrieval systems—without the written permission of the publisher.

LIBRARY OF CONGRESS CATALOGING-IN-PUBLICATION DATA

Lace, William W.
  The Vatican / by William W. Lace.
    p. cm. — (Building history series)
Summary: History of the buildings, occupants, and uses of the Vatican in Rome.
Includes bibliographical references and index.
  ISBN 1-56006-843-4 (hardback : alk. paper)
  1. Architecture—Vatican City. 2. Vatican City—Buildings, structures, etc. [1. Vatican City.]
I. Title. II. Series.
  NA1124.L33 2004
  945.6'34—dc21

2003011218

Printed in the United States of America

Contents

Foreword	6
Important Dates in the Building of the Vatican	8
Introduction	10
Chapter One The Emperors' Hill	13
Chapter Two The Pope's Palace	25
Chapter Three The Greek Cross	38
Chapter Four The Dome	50
Chapter Five The Latin Cross	62
Chapter Six Bernini's Century	90
Chapter Seven Peter's Bones	102
Epilogue	114
Notes	116
For Further Reading	117
Works Consulted	118
Index	121
Picture Credits	127
About the Author	128

Foreword

Throughout history, as civilizations have evolved and prospered, each has produced unique buildings and architectural styles. Combining the need for both utility and artistic expression, a society's buildings, particularly its large-scale public structures, often reflect the individual character traits that distinguish it from other societies. In a very real sense, then, buildings express a society's values and unique characteristics in tangible form. As scholar Anita Abramovitz comments in her book *People and Spaces*, "Our ways of living and thinking—our habits, needs, fear of enemies, aspirations, materialistic concerns, and religious beliefs—have influenced the kinds of spaces that we build and that later surround and include us."

That specific types and styles of structures constitute an outward expression of the spirit of an individual people or era can be seen in the diverse ways that various societies have built palaces, fortresses, tombs, churches, government buildings, sports arenas, public works, and other such monuments. The ancient Greeks, for instance, were a supremely rational people who originated Western philosophy and science, including the atomic theory and the realization that the Earth is a sphere. Their public buildings, epitomized by Athens's magnificent Parthenon temple, were equally rational, emphasizing order, harmony, reason, and above all, restraint.

By contrast, the Romans, who conquered and absorbed the Greek lands, were a highly practical people preoccupied with acquiring and wielding power over others. The Romans greatly admired and readily copied elements of Greek architecture, but modified and adapted them to their own needs. "Roman genius was called into action by the enormous practical needs of a world empire," wrote historian Edith Hamilton. "Rome met them magnificently. Buildings tremendous, indomitable, amphitheaters where eighty thousand could watch a spectacle, baths where three thousand could bathe at the same time."

In medieval Europe, God heavily influenced and motivated the people, and religion permeated all aspects of society, molding people's worldviews and guiding their everyday actions. That spiritual mindset is reflected in the most important medieval structure—the Gothic cathedral—which, in a sense, was a model of heavenly cities. As scholar Anne Fremantle so elegantly phrases it, the cathedrals were "harmonious elevations of stone and glass reaching up to heaven to seek and receive the light [of God]."

Our more secular modern age, in contrast, is driven by the realities of a global economy, advanced technology, and mass communications. Responding to the needs of international trade and the growth of cities housing millions of people, today's builders construct engineering marvels, among them towering skyscrapers of steel and glass, mammoth marine canals, and huge and elaborate rapid transit systems, all of which would have left their ancestors, even the Romans, awestruck.

In examining some of humanity's greatest edifices, Lucent Books' Building History series recognizes this close relationship between a society's historical character and its buildings. Each volume in the series begins with a historical sketch of the people who erected the edifice, exploring their major achievements as well as the beliefs, customs, and societal needs that dictated the variety, functions, and styles of their buildings. A detailed explanation of how the selected structure was conceived, designed, and built, to the extent that this information is known, makes up the majority of the volume.

Each volume in the Lucent Building History series also includes several special features that are useful tools for additional research. A chronology of important dates gives students an overview, at a glance, of the evolution and use of the structure described. Sidebars create a broader context by adding further details on some of the architects, engineers, and construction tools, materials, and methods that made each structure a reality, as well as the social, political, and/or religious leaders and movements that inspired its creation. Useful maps help the reader locate the nations, cities, streets, and individual structures mentioned in the text; and numerous diagrams and pictures illustrate tools and devices that bring to life various stages of construction. Finally, each volume contains two bibliographies, one for student research, the other listing works the author consulted in compiling the book.

Taken as a whole, these volumes, covering diverse ancient and modern structures, constitute not only a valuable research tool, but also a tribute to the human spirit, a fascinating exploration of the dreams, skills, ingenuity, and dogged determination of the great peoples who shaped history.

Important Dates in the Building of the Vatican

ca. 67
Simon Peter crucified near Rome; buried on Vatican Hill.

324
Emperor Constantine begins building the first St. Peter's Basilica on Vatican Hill.

ca. 503
Pope Symmachus is the first to build a residence at the Vatican.

852
The Vatican becomes Leonie City, separate from Rome.

1277
Pope Nicholas III, the first pope to establish permanent residence at the Vatican, begins building what is the oldest part of the present Apostolic Palace.

1490
Belvedere Villa is built for Pope Innocent VIII.

1471–1484
Pope Sixtus IV begins the Vatican Library; builds the Sistine Chapel on the site of earlier chapel of Pope Nicholas III.

200   400   600   800   1000   1200   1300   1400

1145–1216
Popes Eugenius III and Innocent III build the earliest parts of the Apostolic Palace.

ca. 850
Pope Leo IV builds walls around the Vatican.

ca. 170
The *aedicula*, or small shrine, built to the apostle Peter.

1309
Pope Clement V moves the papacy to Avignon, France.

1447–1455
Pope Nicholas V completes the buildings around Papagallo Court.

1417–1431
Pope Martin V begins building the Vatican complex.

1377
Pope Gregory XI returns to Rome; with the Lateran Palace gone, he settles near the Vatican.

1503–1513
Pope Julius II commissions Bramante to build the Court of the Belvedere; finished by Pope Sixtus V (1585–1590).

1520
Sangallo the Younger is appointed chief architect after Raphael's death.

1530
Pope Clement VII crowns Charles V, the last emperor to be crowned at St. Peter's Basilica.

1546
Michelangelo is appointed architect by Pope Paul III.

1588–90
The dome is completed by della Porta. Pope Sixtus V splits the Belvedere courtyard; Fontana builds the papal apartments.

1626
Pope Urban VIII formally inaugurates St. Peter's Basilica on November 18.

ca. 1640
The present boundaries of the Vatican are established, with completion of the walls, under Urban VIII.

| 1500 | 1550 | 1600 | 1650 | 1700 | 1750 | 1800 |

1586
Della Porta moves the obelisk to St. Peter's Square.

1614
Maderno completes the facade St. Peter's Basilica.

1624–1633
Bernini builds the *baldacchino*, the canopy over the high altar.

1506
Pope Julius II lays the cornerstone for the new St. Peter's Basilica.

1929
Pope Pius XI concludes the Lateran Treaty recognizing the Italian republic; Italy indemnifies the papacy for lost land and recognizes Vatican City as a separate state.

1656–66
Bernini builds the colonnade surrounding St. Peter's Square. Bernini builds *cattedra Petri*, or Throne of Peter.

Introduction

Rome, one of the world's great cities, has been called many things, but peaceful and quiet are seldom among them. Yet, across one street, in a plaza, lies a different country. Across the plaza, in a church, lies a different world.

The scene along the sidewalks of the Via della Conciliazione, running west from the Tiber River, is typical. People in animated conversation swarm in amiable confusion past souvenir shops, newsstands, and ice cream vendors. The street itself, like most in the center of Italy's capital, is a rushing torrent of automobiles, their honking horns accompanied by the incessant buzz of motor scooters.

Upon crossing the Via di Porta Angelica, however, one moves within the encircling arms of two gently curving, covered porticos into a plaza. Suddenly the street noise is muted. The traffic disappears. Conversations, boisterous only a moment ago, are subdued.

It is as if, by crossing that short stretch of pavement, one has entered another country. Indeed, this is a different country, though there is no visible borderline and no passport is required. The wall surrounding a complex of buildings and gardens serves as an international boundary. The visitor has left Italy and is now in the City State of the Vatican, an independent nation smaller than New York City's Central Park.

A Spiritual Kingdom

The importance of Vatican City, however, is not to be measured in square miles, for it is here that the pope, supreme head of the Roman Catholic Church, makes his home and headquarters. His political kingdom might be less than a fifth of a square mile, but he is the spiritual ruler of more than 1 billion people—one of every eight on Earth.

The Vatican is a place apart in a sense other than geographical or political. At its center is the immense basilica of St. Peter, its majestic dome dwarfing everything around it. Rome is filled with monumental architecture known around the world, yet something sets St. Peter's apart. Perhaps it is its location, dominating Rome's skyline atop Vatican Hill across the Tiber. Perhaps it is its sheer size. Whatever the reasons St. Peter's stands in Rome like a monarch, part of the great city's surroundings, yet somehow above them.

The sense of separation grows when one crosses the plaza, St. Peter's Square, and enters one of the five huge metal doors that lead into the basilica. Here what seems like another country becomes another world—that of the spiritual.

Immediate Change

The change is immediate. What little outside noise that penetrates the thick walls is quickly swallowed up by the enormous

The immense basilica of St. Peter's, with its intricate facade and towering dome, dominates the architecture of Vatican City.

space within. The light is muted—not so dark as to be gloomy, but rather a soft, soothing radiance in peaceful contrast to the harsh glare of daylight outside. There are plenty of people around—St. Peter's is, after all, the number one tourist attraction in Rome—but they and their voices are diminished by the vastness of the building's interior.

Gradually people make their way toward Gian Lorenzo Bernini's ornate *baldacchino,* or canopy, which sits under the dome designed by Michelangelo. Under the canopy is the high altar of St. Peter's, the heart of the Vatican, at which only the pope can conduct a mass, or religious service.

Two thousand years of tradition dictate much in the Roman Catholic Church, and the most venerated tradition of all governed the placement of the high altar. Directly beneath the dome, the canopy, and the gleaming marble altar is, according to tradition, the tomb of the first pope, Peter, one of the Twelve Apostles of Jesus of Nazareth. And it is beneath these layers, not only of stone and mortar but also of time and tradition, one finds the beginning of the history of the Vatican.

1

THE EMPERORS' HILL

Long before there was a church, there was Vatican Hill. This site would become one of the world's spiritual centers through the actions of two Roman emperors: One was an act of barbaric cruelty; the other, an expression of gratitude and devotion.

In pre-Christian times worshipers of the goddess Cybele held rites on the hill each spring, thus giving the site the name Mons Vaticanus, or Hill of Prophecy. Its only other distinction was the poor quality of the wine produced from grapes growing on the hillside. One poet wrote that if one liked to drink vinegar one would enjoy Vatican wine.

The hill is not one of the traditional seven hills of Rome. Indeed, in Jesus' time it was not considered a part of Rome at all because it

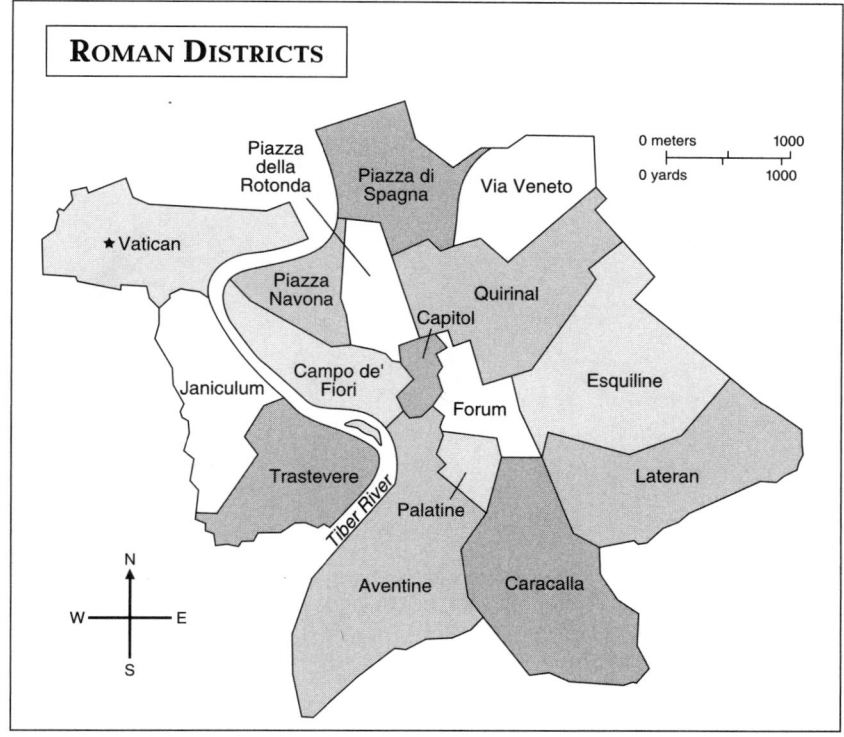

lay outside the city walls, west of the Tiber River, on the road to the port city of Ostia. During the first century A.D., however, the imperial family, seeking relief from the increasingly crowded city, constructed gardens on the hillside.

A few years after Jesus' crucifixion in A.D. 30 the emperor Caligula chose a spot just south of the hill to build a circus, a long, oval amphitheater for chariot races and gladiatorial contests. Building stopped when Caligula was murdered by his troops, but the structure was finished under Nero who was emperor from 54 to 68.

Rome at this time was the center of a vast empire stretching from Britain to Palestine, which was most of the known ancient world. People from every corner of the empire came to Rome, bringing their various religions with them. Among the dozens of sects was the small band of Christians, followers of Jesus of Nazareth. Their leader was Simon Peter who had arrived in Rome about A.D. 42.

A drawing shows the amphitheater of Nero, built near Vatican hill, flooded with water to reenact a sea battle.

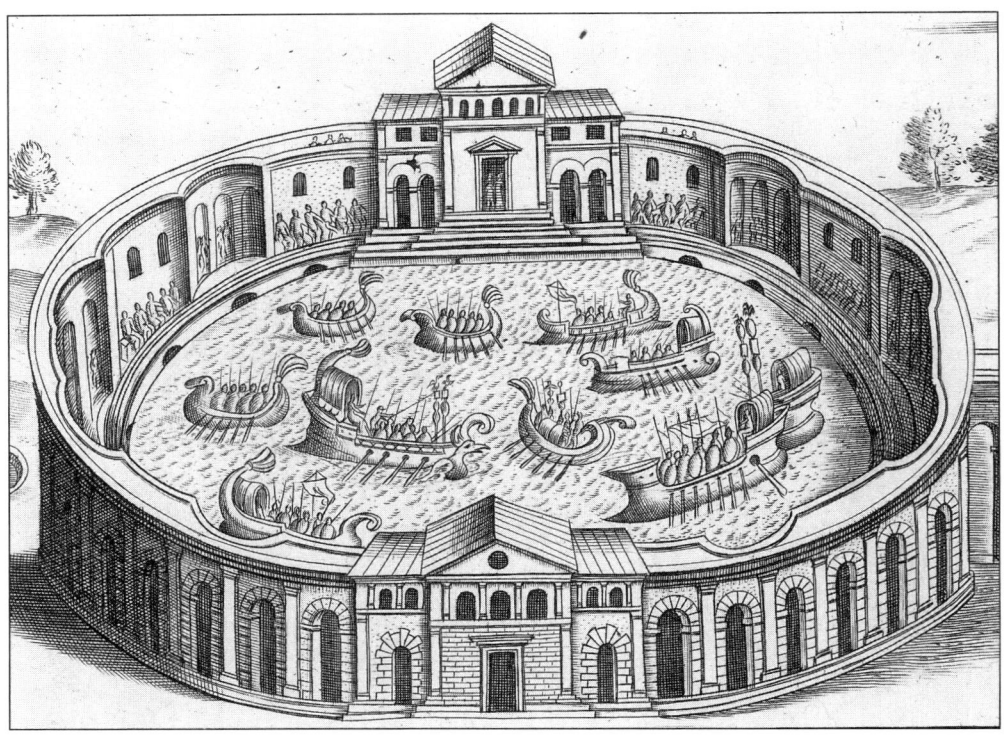

PETER

Peter was born Simon bar Jonah in Galilee, a part of the Roman province of Palestine. A rough-mannered, uneducated fisherman, he had been chosen by Jesus to be one of his Twelve Apostles, or followers. Jesus had recognized his qualities of leadership, and Peter became a leader among the apostles.

In a passage from the New Testament's Book of Matthew in the Bible, Jesus asks his apostles who they think him to be. Simon speaks up saying that he believes Jesus to be the Christ, the prophesied Messiah, or Savior—the Son of God. Jesus tells Simon that God has revealed this to him and that henceforth he shall be known as Peter, from the Greek *petros,* or rock. Peter, Jesus says, will be the rock on which his earthly church will be built.

Furthermore, Jesus says in chapter 6, verse 19 of the Book of Matthew he gives Peter the "keys to the kingdom" with authority to admit people into or exclude them from heaven after death. Jesus is not quoted in Scripture specifically as saying that Peter's successors would have similar authority, but the Roman Catholic Church maintains that this was his intent—that Jesus did not mean to confer only temporary authority in one middle-aged man. This belief in the handing of spiritual power from person to person, known as the Apostolic Succession, is the bedrock on which the papacy is founded.

This 1472 painting depicts Saint Peter with the "keys to the kingdom" given to him by Jesus.

During Peter's ministry in Rome, Christians were drawn mostly from the lower classes—laborers, slaves, and former slaves. They were set apart from the many other religions, however, by their refusal—frequently public and loud—to acknowledge the divinity of the emperor and to sacrifice to him. Emperor Claudius expelled them in 49, and they were not allowed to return until 56.

PETER THE MAN

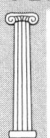

The man in whose honor the Vatican was built was a simple Jewish fisherman before being chosen by Jesus of Nazareth to be one of his Twelve Apostles. Peter was born Simon bar Jonah but was given the name Peter, from the Greek word for "rock," when Jesus declared that he would be the foundation of Jesus' earthly kingdom, the church.

In the Bible the gospels of Matthew, Mark, Luke, and John, and the Acts of the Apostles, give Peter a much more sharply defined personality than any of the other disciples. He is portrayed as a down-to-earth, highly emotional man who could be impetuous to the point of rashness, filled with doubts, bold one minute and cowardly the next.

When Jesus foretells his own death, Peter objects and is told in chapter 16, verse 23 of the Book of Matthew, "Get thee behind me, Satan." On the night Jesus is arrested, Peter forgets his master's message of peace, whips out a sword, and cuts off the ear of one of the high priest's servants. And yet, on the very same night, he denies three times that he even knows who Jesus is.

Peter is an intensely human character and one conscious of his own human frailties. Long after Jesus' death, when Peter has become leader of the church, a Roman officer, Cornelius, falls to his knees in front of him. "Stand up," says Peter. "I myself also am a man."

THE GREAT FIRE

In July of 64 a disastrous fire burned one-third of Rome and damaged another third. Nero, instead of replacing a large section of lost homes, began building a sumptuous palace for himself. The people grumbled and began spreading rumors that Nero had started the great fire himself and on purpose.

The emperor sought to shift the blame and settled on the Christians, accusing them of starting the fire. They were made to suffer publicly and horribly. Nero probably would have preferred to stage public punishments in the huge Circus Maximus, but it had been damaged by the fire. So he had to settle for the smaller amphitheater at the foot of Vatican Hill.

The Christians were rounded up by the hundreds and sent to their deaths before cheering crowds in the amphitheater. Some were torn apart by wild beasts, such a lions. Others were crucified—hung on a cross and left to die. When the sun began to set, others were tied to stakes, smeared with tar, and set ablaze, as the Roman historian Tacitus wrote, "so as to serve the purpose of lamps when daylight failed."[1] Peter was among those crucified. According to tradition he protested that he was unworthy to be put to death in the same manner as Jesus and, at his request, was crucified head downwards. Afterward, according to custom, his body was given to friends who supposedly carried it for burial to a nearby cemetery on the southern slope of Vatican Hill. There was no tomb, and if the grave was marked in any way its location remained a secret for generations. Only a select few of the faithful, to whom Peter remained a sanctified figure as a martyr and founder of the Christian Church, knew of its location.

Gaius's "Trophy"

Sometime in the late 100s a small memorial was erected on Peter's burial spot. The priest Gaius wrote around the end of the century, "If you go to the Vatican or to the Ostian Way [the road to Ostia], you will find the trophies [monuments] of those who founded this church."[2]

The shrine to Peter was built into the west wall of a small courtyard and faced east. It had three niches arranged vertically. The upper niche was a recessed area that rested on a ledge supported by two pillars. Below it, just above ground level, was a second niche. A small marble slab was fitted into the pavement just in front of the shrine. Beneath the slab, it was thought, was the grave containing the body of Peter. The third niche, discovered much later, was below ground and carved out of the base of the wall.

Centuries passed. Waves of persecution of Christians came and went, but the movement grew steadily. The cemetery grew also, as more Christians sought their final resting place near where they thought Peter lay.

Constantine

The turning point for the Vatican, and for Christianity, came in the early 300s with the reign of Emperor Constantine. An army officer and son of a former deputy emperor, Constantine was proclaimed emperor by his troops while stationed in Britain. To claim his throne he had to march on Rome in 312 to face a rival, Maxentius.

Tradition holds that one day, while on the march, he saw a vision—a cross against the midday sun and the words "*In hoc signo vinces,*" Latin for "By this sign you will conquer." The next day he had the Greek letters *chi* and *rho,* the first two letters of the name Christ, inscribed on his soldiers' shields. Constantine went on to win a decisive victory in the battle near Rome, and Maxentius drowned in the Tiber.

Historians have debated the extent to which Constantine was a Christian. Certainly he was no saint, ruthlessly eliminating his rivals and even having his wife strangled when he suspected her loyalty. Yet it was clear that he believed he owed his throne to the Christian God. In 313 he issued the Edict of Milan, which proclaimed religious toleration and ended the persecution of the Christians. He presided over the Council of Nicea in 325 at which Christianity was proclaimed the official religion of the Roman Empire.

This thirteenth-century fresco shows the emperor Constantine donating to the church. Constantine was the first Roman emperor to embrace Christianity and he built the original church on Vatican Hill.

THE EDICT OF MILAN

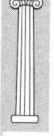

After Constantine won the Battle of Milvian Bridge and became emperor of Rome, he acknowledged the legitimacy not only of Christianity but of all religions. Along with his brother-in-law Licinius, emperor of the eastern part of the Roman Empire, he issued the Edict of Toleration, also known as the Edict of Milan, from the city from which it was decreed.

The Edict of Milan was a remarkable document in that it went completely against the religious bigotry of the time. "It is one thing," Constantine wrote, "to enter voluntarily upon the struggle for immortality, another to compel others to do so from fear of punishment."

The document proclaimed that all persons should be free to believe in whatever they wished, provided that they did not, in the course of these beliefs, infringe on others. "No person," the edict said, "shall molest another; everyone shall keep in check the dictates of his heart . . . no one may, through his convictions, do harm to another."

The excerpts from the edict can be found in James Lees-Milne's *St. Peter's*.

Constantine also showed his gratitude by building two huge christian churches. One was St. John Lateran, next to the palace of his executed wife. The other, dedicated to Peter, was on Vatican Hill.

CHOOSING THE SITE

Although no written record concerning Peter's tomb between the time of Gaius and Constantine has been found, enough knowledge of the location apparently had been preserved to point Constantine to the site on which he decreed the church be built. Furthermore Constantine determined that the altar would be positioned directly over the apostle's grave.

Constantine must have been convinced that Peter was buried on the hillside, for alternative sites such as the level ground of Nero's circus were far more suitable and would have made the task much easier. The first obstacle to overcome was ethical. Over time the cemetery had expanded into a necropolis, a street of mausoleums leading up the incline of the hill. It was strictly against Roman custom to disturb a tomb, yet the entire cemetery had to be destroyed to create the huge level area needed to support Constantine's church.

A second obstacle involved engineering challenges. To create a level surface large enough for the giant structure, Constantine's builders had to remove not only the tombs from the western slope above the site of Peter's burial, but also tons of earth beneath them. On the eastern slope, below Peter's grave, workers cut the roofs from the rows of tombs and filled in the cemetery with the earth taken from the western side. Tradition says that the emperor carried the first twelve basketfuls of earth on his own shoulders, one for each of Jesus' twelve apostles, symbolizing his dedication of the church to the god who had given him victory.

The result was a space 750 feet long from east to west and four hundred feet wide from south to north. This space dictated not only the shape of Constantine's church—the first St. Peter's—but also the structure that would replace it more than a thousand years later. This second church—still called by some the "new" St. Peter's, even though it was begun five hundred years ago—is the one that stands today.

Facing East

Most ancient churches—Christian and pre-Christian—were aligned east–west to take advantage of the effect of light from the rising sun. Customarily, churches were entered at the western end, opening into the nave, the long chamber where worshipers stood or knelt. However, the entrance and nave of St. Peter's is at the eastern end. Historians suggest that it was easier, given the slope of Vatican Hill, to put the longer portion of the church on the east side. Perhaps, also, it was designed in this way so the entrance would face Rome.

The names of the first St. Peter's architects are unknown, but they followed a design customary in early Christian churches. It was modeled on the basilica, or Roman law court, and retained the name even though built for another purpose.

The basilica, the style of which the Romans had copied from ancient Greek models, was part of the forum, or business and judicial center, of every Roman city. Outside was a large courtyard. Inside the basilica was also large and open, so that all citizens could witness court proceedings. The building was rectangular—about twice as long as it was wide. At the end opposite the entrance was a semicircular recess known as the apse. In the center of the apse was a cathedra, or throne, from which the Roman judge dispensed justice. As the basilica was transformed into a church, the cathedra became the bishop's throne, thus giving the name cathedral to any church presided over by the high-ranking clergyman called a bishop.

The altar—now honoring the Christian God rather than the pre-Christian Minerva, goddess of wisdom—was placed between the bishop and the congregation, usually on a raised platform situated over the sacred remains of a saint, Peter in this case. The entire area from apse to altar was called the chancel, from the

Constantine's basilica is depicted in this fresco, with its long nave and altar placed over the reputed tomb of St. Peter.

cancelli, a low divider that in Roman times separated the judge and his assistants from the public. At first the chancel contained only the clergy and altar. Later, singers were installed on either side of the aisle between the altar and the chancel rail, and their area became the choir.

THE BASILICA OF CONSTANTINE

Worshipers reached the basilica built by Constantine by climbing thirty-five steps, crossing a two-hundred-foot-long courtyard, and entering one of five doors. The interior was 360 feet long by 180 feet wide, separated into five aisles by four rows of columns. The focal point was the small shrine believed to mark Peter's original grave. The grave was not beneath an altar but at pavement level,

POWERS OF THE SHRINE

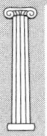

When Constantine constructed his basilica, the shrine of Peter, erected about 150 years earlier, stood in the western end in the center of the apse. It was encased in marble and surrounded by a low railing in the shape of a square.

At each corner of the square stood four columns of unusual design—twisted instead of straight, with alternating stages of fluting and carved vines. The columns had been brought from Greece and the legend grew up that they had once been part of Solomon's Temple in Jerusalem, destroyed by the Romans in A.D. 70.

Shortly before A.D. 600 Pope Gregory I encased the shrine in a marble altar. Before then, however, it was thought to have special powers. Priests would unlock a door in the back of the marble casing, revealing a small window. Pilgrims placing their heads through the window would have whatever they wished for granted, provided they were righteous and the wish was something in accordance with God's will.

The pilgrims then withdrew their heads and dropped a piece of cloth, hanging from a string, into the tomb below the shrine. They waited, sometimes praying and fasting for hours, then brought the cloth back to the surface. If they had found favor with God, the cloth would be much heavier, having soaked in the sanctity of Peter's spirit, and could be used to work miracles.

covered with a much more elaborate structure—a canopy resting on four marble pillars. A mosaic floor covered the marble slab, thus sealing off what was believed to be the actual grave.

Most pillars in Greek and Roman architecture were straight and smooth, but the pillars supporting St. Peter's canopy were twisted into spiral shapes and covered with carvings of vines in imitation of the pillars of the ancient Jewish temple of Solomon in Jerusalem. The pillars and one of the five doors would be among the very few items to be incorporated into the new St. Peter's centuries later.

In 594 Pope Gregory I raised the floor around the shrine, which could still be viewed from the front through a grill and could still be reached from behind by a passageway underneath the new pavement. A highly decorated space was hollowed out of the upper part of the back of the shrine and designated the Niche of the Pallia, in which new archbishops still place their *pallia,* or mantles of office, the night before their consecration.

Gregory also placed an altar on the raised floor, immediately over the tomb, incorporating the top of the wall into which Peter's shrine had been built. The lower part and the site of the grave were paved over and out of sight. The basilica would remain essentially unchanged from this point for almost nine hundred years.

DECLINE OF ROME

Constantine had hardly finished building St. Peter's before abandoning Rome, transferring his capital east to Constantinople, formerly Byzantium. Rome began to decline, suffering invasions by Germanic tribes in the mid-500s and by Islamic pirates, called Saracens, in 846. The Saracen invasion caused the reigning pope, Leo IV, to begin what would become Vatican City by building walls to enclose the area.

The papacy reached its peak of power in 1077 when Henry IV, emperor of the Holy Roman Empire, humbled himself before Pope Gregory VII. Gradually, however, the secular rulers of Europe acquired powers rivaling those of the church and no longer looked to Rome for supreme authority. Kings openly challenged the popes and one, King Philip IV of France, arranged the election of a French cardinal as pope and in 1309 moved the papacy to the French city of Avignon.

There would be no popes in Rome for almost seventy years, a period in church history known as the Babylonian Captivity. St. Peter's, which had been in urgent need of repair for many years, was virtually abandoned. Wolves came through gaps in the Vatican walls to dig in the cemetery for recently buried bodies. The walls of the basilica were near collapse. Cows grazed on grass growing between the paving stones of the courtyard and even wandered into the church itself.

It was clear that a new St. Peter's would have to be built. The popes were busy, however, with other matters—wars, and a split within the church—that occupied their time and emptied their purses. The start of a new church in tribute to the man crucified fourteen hundred years before would have to wait yet another century.

2

THE POPE'S PALACE

When the papacy returned to Rome after seventy years in France, church officials found old St. Peter's in serious disrepair. Something, probably a new church, was clearly required. But before they built a place to pray, the popes needed a place to live. The next century would see little work on the basilica and much more on the Apostolic Palace, the name generally given to the buildings housing the popes' living quarters, ceremonial rooms, and the vast Vatican museums.

The Vatican, indeed, had never been the permanent papal residence. Symmachus, pope from 498 to 515, built some kind of dwelling next to the basilica after being driven out of Rome by a rival. This structure was enlarged for the crowning of Charlemagne as Holy Roman Emperor in 800 and became a guest palace for Charlemagne's successors, who received their crowns at the hands of the popes.

The popes stayed for brief periods in the Vatican, but their permanent home was the Lateran Palace, which had been the home of Constantine's wife. After having her executed, the emperor gave the palace to the church, perhaps in atonement for what he had done. He built the Church of St. John next to the dwelling, and the popes took up residence in the Lateran Palace, preferring its relative safety inside the city walls to the vulnerability of the unprotected and unfortified buildings at the Vatican. When Pope Gregory XI, and thus the papacy, returned from France to Rome in 1377, however, there was no Lateran Palace. It had burned in 1308.

Gregory and his successors did have a roof over their heads, though, thanks to the efforts of some popes in the 1100s and 1200s. Pope Eugenius III had begun building a palace north of St. Peter's Basilica in about 1150. Later popes made small additions throughout the second half of the century, but it was Nicholas III, pope from 1277 to 1280, who began construction of what visitors see today as the Apostolic Palace.

THE PAPPAGALLO

Nicholas began building on either side of Eugenius's palace. His plan was to construct a square palace surrounding a courtyard,

Pope Gregory XI, shown here in this fifteenth-century painting, returned the papacy to Rome in 1377 and initiated a renovation of the Vatican site, beginning with its palaces.

and he completed the southern and eastern sides before his death. The square palace, surrounding the court nicknamed the Pappagallo, or parrot, because some now-vanished statues of mythological birds once existed there, would not be finished for more than 170 years, seventy years after the popes returned from France.

Nicholas's additions to the palace reflected the uncertainty of the times in which it was built. The walls are sheer and unadorned; windows are small. The overall impression was that of a fortress, which in effect is what it was. Far distant was the time when popes could feel free from attack. Nicholas even built a covered passage leading from the palace to the huge Castle of San Angelo, situated near the banks of the Tiber, so that he would have an escape route—one that several future popes would find both convenient and necessary.

Nicholas's contributions to the Vatican went beyond his palace. He strengthened the Vatican walls begun by Pope Leo IV. He also expended huge sums from his treasury to buy large parcels of nearby land, thus establishing the future boundaries of Vatican City.

The years following the papacy's return from France were anything but peaceful. What historians have termed the Great Western Schism split the church as first two and then three rival popes were elected, each claiming absolute authority and each backed by rival rulers and their armies. Consequently little building occurred at the Vatican. One pope, Eugenius IV, did commission a great bronze door subsequently used when the basilica was rebuilt.

Pope Nicholas V

The papacy was finally reunited under Pope Martin V in 1417, but it was not until Pope Nicholas V in 1447 that building on the Apostolic Palace resumed in earnest. He rebuilt the palace of Pope Nicholas III and added the wings on the northern and western sides, thus completing the square palace surrounding the Pappagallo. Pope Nicholas V also added to the defensive fortifications, constructing the tower, later named for him, on the southernmost corner of the Vatican wall. He announced plans to rebuild St. Peter's but was only able to restore some of the old basilica before he died.

Building was only one of Nicholas V's interests. He was an avid book collector, and his collection formed the beginnings of the Vatican Library, eventually one of the world's finest. He admired artists, calling them "keepers or guardians on the earth of the eternal verities [truths]."[3] Renaissance painting was just beginning to come into full flower in Italy, and Nicholas invited such painters as Fra Angelico, who decorated the pope's private chapel, to work in the Vatican.

Sixtus IV (1471–1484) was a pope much in the same mold as Nicholas V. He officially established the Vatican Library, installing it in four rooms on the first floor of the northern side of the palace and opening it to the public. He is best remembered, however, for the great chapel—the Sistine Chapel—he built to the west of the palace alongside and parallel to the basilica.

THE SISTINE CHAPEL

This chapel, named Sistine in honor of Pope Sixtus IV, was constructed on the site of an earlier one built by Pope Nicholas III. The newer structure was 133 feet by 44 feet on the interior, exactly the same dimensions as Solomon's Temple in Jerusalem that was destroyed by Romans in A.D. 70. While the outside of the

THE VATICAN LIBRARY

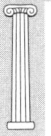

Every day, tourists troop through the Vatican museums to gaze at some of the world's greatest works of art. Less well known and much less frequently seen is another collection perhaps even more impressive, the Vatican Library.

Pope Nicholas V, under whom significant portions of the Apostolic Palace were built, founded the library. On his death in 1455, his collection included about eleven hundred Greek and Latin codices, books of parchment leaves bound together, usually containing religious scripture.

The physical library to house the collection, which quickly grew to more than twenty-five hundred volumes, was built by Pope Sixtus IV. It consisted of four rooms on the north side of the Pappagallo Court and was dedicated on June 15, 1475.

The rooms quickly became too small, and Pope Sixtus V commissioned Domenico Fontana to build a new library between the two long corridors to the east and west of the Court of the Belvedere.

Today the Vatican Library is one of the world's finest. It contains more than seventy-five thousand codices and about eighty-two thousand incunabula, the earliest printed books. In all, the library contains more than eight hundred thousand works.

chapel was as grim and forbidding as the rest of the Apostolic Palace, the inside was designed by Sixtus as a vast area on the surfaces of which the finest painters of the time—Perugino, Boticelli, Ghirlandaio, and Cosimo Roseselli—painted scenes from the Bible. The greatest glory of the Sistine Chapel, however, would have to wait for another century, another pope, and another artist.

In the meantime there would be two more significant additions to the Apostolic Palace. The first came under Pope Innocent VIII (1484–1492), who found the medieval fortress so depressing that he decided to build new quarters as far away from it as possible while remaining in the Vatican. He commissioned a residence to be constructed eight hundred yards away from the old palace in the northeast corner of the ancient wall.

His retreat, named the Belvedere, or "beautiful view," because of its position higher on the slope of Vatican Hill, was modeled after the ancient Roman villas. Open, airy, and inviting, it was a complete departure from the grim medieval palace. It was the first villa in the old style built since the days of the Roman empire and would be widely imitated throughout Italy and the rest of Europe during the Renaissance.

The Borgia Tower

Back to the south the old palace took on an even more formidable look with construction of the Borgia Tower on the northwest corner. It was built by Pope Alexander VI, a member of the Spanish Borgia family and possibly the most immoral ruler in the history of the Vatican. Several Renaissance popes were more worldly than pious, but Alexander—with his illegitimate children and rumored assassinations of enemies—shocked even the tolerant Italians.

Alexander's other contribution was the decoration of the Borgia Apartments, four rooms on the first floor of the northern wing of the palace. Even though covered with masterworks by the artist Pinturicchio, these rooms were shunned by future popes because of the reputation of their founder. It was even rumored that the ghost of the pope's murdered son walked there at night.

Julius II, who perhaps had the greatest influence of any pope on the Vatican, was elected in 1503, three months after Alexander's death. While much of his attention went to the rebuilding of St. Peter's Basilica, he did not neglect the Apostolic Palace. As a result, visitors today can see there some of the greatest works of art ever executed.

30 THE VATICAN

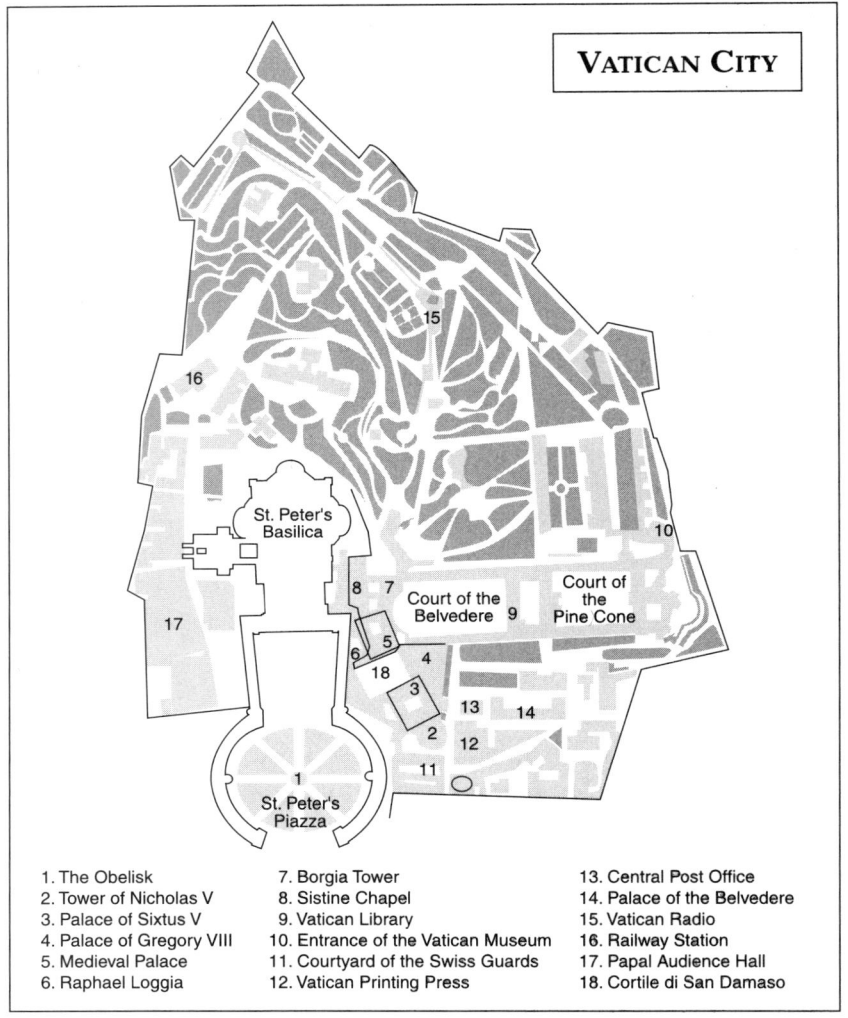

1. The Obelisk
2. Tower of Nicholas V
3. Palace of Sixtus V
4. Palace of Gregory VIII
5. Medieval Palace
6. Raphael Loggia
7. Borgia Tower
8. Sistine Chapel
9. Vatican Library
10. Entrance of the Vatican Museum
11. Courtyard of the Swiss Guards
12. Vatican Printing Press
13. Central Post Office
14. Palace of the Belvedere
15. Vatican Radio
16. Railway Station
17. Papal Audience Hall
18. Cortile di San Damaso

THE SISTINE CEILING

Pope Julius greatly admired the *Pietà*, the sculpture of Mary holding the crucified Jesus done in 1499 by the brilliant young Michelangelo Buonarroti. In 1505 Julius commissioned Michelangelo to carve the pope's tomb, a tremendous work to include forty life-sized and larger-than-life statues. After the artist spent considerable time and money acquiring marble and setting up a shop, Julius changed his mind. He now asked Michelangelo to redecorate the ceiling of the Sistine Chapel, which had been built by his uncle.

Michelangelo protested that he was a sculptor, not a painter, but Julius, used to having his way, made the request a command. Michelangelo, however, was just as stubborn as the pope. Rather than submit, he fled from Rome to his home city of Florence. Julius sent envoys to bring him back. Michelangelo refused. The pope demanded the government of Florence return the artist to Rome. The Florentines urged Michelangelo to obey, but he said that he would rather leave Italy altogether and work for the sultan of Turkey.

Finally, in 1506, Michelangelo reluctantly bowed to the pope's wishes, but it was not until 1508 that work on the ceiling began. He would use a technique known as fresco, from the Italian word

WATCHING AND WAITING

The Sistine Chapel is a place for worship and prayer, but it also is where perhaps the most dramatic events at the Vatican take place. Here, beneath Michelangelo's fabulous frescoed ceiling, the College of Cardinals meets to elect a new pope.

The meeting is called a conclave, a combination of the two Latin words for "with" and "key." The cardinals are literally locked in the Apostolic Palace until one of them is elected pope.

Church law recognizes three methods of election: inspiration, where the choice is so obvious the candidate is elected by acclamation; compromise, through a series of negotiations; or scrutiny, a secret ballot requiring a two-thirds majority.

The secret ballot has been the method most often used. After each round of voting, the ballots are burned. If no pope has been elected, damp straw is mixed with the paper so that black smoke issues from the chimney above the chapel. Below, in St. Peter's Square, thousands gather to watch.

When a pope is finally elected—and sometimes it has taken weeks—white smoke signals to the crowd that Peter has a new successor. The new pope retires to a special room in the palace, the Room of Tears, to dress in the white papal robes before appearing on the balcony to the cheers of the faithful.

for "fresh," in which paint was applied to damp plaster. When the paint dried, the colors were embedded in the plaster rather than merely put on the surface.

Julius's idea was to divide the ceiling into twelve panels and paint one of Jesus' apostles in each. Michelangelo convinced the pope that the ceiling's irregular contour would make such a scheme impractical. Instead he suggested nine rectangular panels, each with a scene from the Old Testament, surrounded by paintings of Biblical prophets Jesus' ancestors, and nude male figures.

This painting shows Pope Julius II commissioning Michelangelo to redecorate sections of the Vatican.

God, as depicted by Michelangelo in the Creation of Adam *on the ceiling of the Sistine Chapel, has become one of the most recognizable images in art history.*

MICHELANGELO'S CHALLENGES

Michelangelo worked for four years, sometimes aided by assistants but often alone, high on a special scaffold he had designed so as not to leave holes in the ceiling or the walls. His other problem was artistic rather than mechanical—how to paint large figures on a curved surface which, when seen from almost seventy feet below, would appear in proportion.

Michelangelo apparently solved the perspective problem as he went. The earlier scenes—he worked from Noah backward in biblical time—appear crowded. The later ones are big and bold, masterful and majestic. The image of God reaching out to give the touch of life to Adam is perhaps the most famous image in all of art. Little wonder that, when the chapel was opened to the public on November 1, 1512, it caused—as contemporary artist Gregorio Vasari wrote—"the wonder and astonishment of the whole of Rome."[4] The ceiling still astonishes the approximately 5 million tourists who view it each year.

Michelangelo might have been finished with the Sistine ceiling, but not with the chapel itself. Twenty-four years after the ceiling was completed, Pope Paul III asked him to do a fresco for the large wall behind the altar. As he had with Julius II, Michelangelo tried to decline. Paul would have none of it. He had been attempting, long before becoming pope, to engage Michelangelo in a project. The usually placid Paul thundered, "I have wanted this for thirty years, and now that I am pope will you not satisfy me?"[5] Michelangelo, as before, bowed to the papal will.

His theme was the Last Judgment—the final reckoning at which Jesus decides the fate of humankind. This time for the artist there was no hesitation, no learning. The commanding figure of Jesus dominates the huge (forty-four by forty-eight feet) painting. Lesser figures swirl around him in a whirlpool of color. Those who are saved ascend into heaven where angels sound golden trumpets. Those who are damned are dragged down to hell by leering demons.

Michelangelo's Influence

Michelangelo's work, specifically the Sistine ceiling, had an enormous influence on another great artist of the time, Rafaello Sanzio, generally known as Raphael. He was working at the Apostolic Palace at the same time as Michelangelo, having been commissioned by Julius II to decorate his private apartments.

Though not as well known as the Sistine Chapel works, Raphael's Stanze, three rooms in which Julius lived and worked, are masterpieces in their own right. Of the three—nicknamed Signatura, Heliodorus, and The Borgio Fire—the Signatura is the most important. It is mostly the work of the master, whereas much of the painting in the other rooms was done by assistants. In the Signatura is found Raphael's famous *School of Athens,* a fresco celebrating human intellect in which the most famous thinkers of history—philosophers Aristotle and Plato, mathematician Euclid, astronomer Ptolemy—are gathered.

The influence of Michelangelo on Raphael was immediately obvious. Vasari wrote that Raphael, "who was very excellent in imitation . . . changed his manner."[6] Indeed, portions of the Stanze painted after the opening of the Sistine Chapel show how Raphael began to copy Michelangelo's style.

The Loggia

Julius II, however, was not interested only in painting. His other great contribution to the Apostolic Palace was architectural. He appointed Donato Bramante to design both a new St. Peter's, an effort to be discussed later, as well as additions to the palace. One addition was a three-story series of loggia—open-sided, roofed galleries running along the eastern side looking out over the Tiber toward Rome.

Bramante's design was highly original and one of the first examples of true Renaissance architecture to be incorporated in the Vatican. Originally the three loggia consisted of arches, but Raphael altered the plan after Bramante's death, changing the third story by using light columns. Furthermore Raphael decorated the interior walls and ceilings of the loggia with Biblical scenes, some of which also showed Michelangelo's influence.

Bramante's other project was to connect the main body of the palace with the Belvedere Villa to the north. His plan, which would take more than fifty years to complete, was to construct two long parallel arms extending north from the medieval palace to the villa. To do so he had to put a new facade on the villa to

AN ARTIST'S JOKE

The painting by Michelangelo of *The Last Judgment* behind the altar of the Sistine Chapel was not without its humorous moments. One of Pope Paul III's servants, Biagio da Cesena, who saw the work before it was finished, complained about the nude figures, calling them indecent.

Da Cesena complained so often and so loudly that Michelangelo replied by giving one of the horned devils driving condemned souls into hell features remarkably like those of the troublesome official. Da Cesena was furious and complained to the pope.

Paul came to look at the painting and, suppressing a smile, told his servant, as quoted in *The World of Michelangelo* by Robert Coughlan, "Had the painter sent you to purgatory [halfway between heaven and hell], I would use my best efforts to get you released; but I exercise no influence in Hell; there you are beyond redemption."

Michelangelo's enemies had some measure of revenge fifteen years later when another pope, Paul IV, objected to the nudes. Daniele da Volterra, one of Michelangelo's assistants, was given the job of painting veils and drapes over the offending parts and was known thereafter as Il Braghettone, "The Britches Maker."

make it parallel with the old palace and thus form a rectangle. He built it as a replica of the Roman ruins at Palestrina. The facade features a semicircular space, called the Great Niche, in which was placed the huge carving of a pine cone that had once stood in the atrium of the basilica.

The facade, two stories of the three-story eastern arm, and the foundations of the western arm were completed before Bramante died in 1514. The project languished but was finally finished under Pope Pius IV in about 1560. The huge rectangle thus formed was named the Court of the Belvedere and became the site of some distinctly irreligious activities, such as jousting and bullfights.

DIVIDING THE COURT

Pope Sixtus V (1585–1590) took a dim view of sporting events taking place within the Vatican. He divided the Court of the Belvedere by constructing a new wing running east–west that split the court-

This sixteenth-century engraving shows a jousting tournament in the Court of the Belvedere. Such irreligious activities were common in the courtyard after its construction in 1560.

yard in half. The southern part, still called the Court of the Belvedere, is now a parking lot. The northern part became known as the Court of the Pine Cone.

Other popes had made other additions. Pius V (1566–1572) built a series of chapels along the northwest corner of the Court of the Belvedere. Gregory XIII (1572–1585) built a wing connecting the medieval palace to the Tower of Nicholas V. At various times loggia much like those of Bramante and Raphael were added to relieve the starkness of the medieval facade. Most of the loggia have since been glassed in to protect the paintings inside.

Sixtus V—the same pope who split the courtyard—made the last truly significant addition to the palace. He commissioned architect Domenico Fontana to build a new palace, a large square next to the Tower of Nicholas V. The new building connected with Gregory XIII's wing, thus forming a new square named the Court of Saint Damascus. The palace of Sixtus V is the present site of the pope's private apartments. From a window on the third floor the pope gives his blessing each Sunday to throngs of the faithful gathered in St. Peter's Square.

There would eventually be many more additions to the Vatican other than to the palace or St. Peter's. Most occurred in the twentieth century and include such functional facilities as the pope's modern auditorium, a railroad station, a radio station, office buildings, and the quarters of the pope's Swiss Guards in their colorful medieval uniforms.

The time, efforts, and fortunes of generations of popes and architects went into the building of the Apostolic Palace. Yet, grand as it eventually became, the palace was always considered secondary to the basilica. It was not until the palace was well on its way to completion, however, that major work began on St. Peter's, and once more it was that most energetic of popes, Julius II, who provided the spark.

3

THE GREEK CROSS

The papacy had no sooner recovered from the Babylonian Captivity and the Great Western Schism than the popes set their eyes on the rebuilding of the crumbling St. Peter's Basilica begun by Emperor Constantine. However, it would be fifty years before the iron will of Pope Julius II turned dreams into action and another fifty years until the genius of Michelangelo gave it permanent form. Even then, a century after Pope Nicholas V first determined to rebuild the church, it was still another half century from being finished.

Soon after Nicholas became pope in 1447, his architect, Leon Battista Alberti, warned him that the south wall of the old basilica was leaning to the extent that any slight shock would cause it to collapse. Yet, even though Nicholas said that "noble edifice . . . would immensely conduce [lead] to the exaltation of the Chair of St. Peter,"[7] his work was mainly on the palace instead of the basilica.

Nicholas did have Alberti's associate, Bernardo Rossellino, draw up a plan for a new church, however. It was remarkably similar to the existing building—a square atrium leading into a nave with five aisles—but featured a dome over the altar. The only part begun was the new choir and apse—the Tribuna di San Piero—which would eventually give way to a later plan. The walls of the choir were six feet high by 1455 when Nicholas died.

Neither of the next two popes, Calixtus III nor Pius II, were much interested in building, and it was not until Pope Paul II that more was done. In 1470 he engaged Giuliano da Sangallo, who had worked for the Medici family in Florence, to complete the choir, but Paul died less than a year later and work stopped once more.

MAKING REPAIRS

Paul's successor, Pope Sixtus IV, is best known for commissioning the Sistine Chapel but was much more interested in keeping old St. Peter's from falling down than in building a new one. He braced the walls, restored the roof, put in more windows and repaved the floor. He also built a new ciborium, or canopy, over the site of Peter's tomb that was to last for the next 150 years. Likewise, Pope Innocent VIII (1484–1492) is known much more for having the Belvedere built and Pope Alexander VI (1492–1503) for the Borgia Apartments than for any construction they undertook at St. Peter's.

Finally, fifty years and six popes after Nicholas V voiced an intention to rebuild St. Peter's, the project found a person who would spur it toward completion. Pope Julius II (1503–1513) was a man with bold ideas, the sense of action to carry them through, and the strength of will to overcome obstacles. He bent Michelangelo to his will over the Sistine ceiling and he would do the same with the Romans and church officials who had formed an attachment to the old St. Peter's and did not want it replaced.

Not only the pope, but also the time was right for a major reconstruction of St. Peter's. Some of Julius II's immediate predecessors simply did not have the money. Julius had no such problem.

A painting of Pope Sixtus IV giving a mass in the Sistine Chapel. Sixtus commissioned the chapel that bears his name.

Silver and gold were beginning to flow from the New World to Europe, and plenty found its way into the Vatican treasury.

Julius chose as the man to carry out his grand plan a seasoned architect named Donato Bramante, who had worked for him early in his papacy. Bramante was just as forceful as Julius but lacked the pope's thoroughness. He was highly impatient, and his lack of supervision of work on both St. Peter's and the palace would lead to expensive repairs afterward.

INDULGENCES

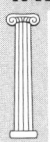

It is one of the great ironies of history that the building of St. Peter's Basilica, center of the Roman Catholic faith, was indirectly the cause of the Protestant Reformation that split Christian Europe in two. The factor linking the two was the sale of indulgences.

According to Roman Catholic doctrine, it is possible for someone who has committed a sin to go beyond confessing the sin and, through an act of repentance, be granted an indulgence. Indulgences are based, in part, on the idea that Jesus took the sins of humanity on himself and thus built up a "treasury" of forgiveness.

According to Roman Catholic doctrine, sinners can draw on that treasury, if sanctioned by church authority, through prayer, fasting, or the giving of alms, which are donations to God. Such acts, in effect, pay a debt to God and lessen the time one's soul must spend in purgatory before sins are wiped out and the soul may proceed to heaven.

When Pope Julius II in 1513 needed money for the building of St. Peter's, however, he let it be known that indulgences would be given to those who contributed money to the project. Agents of the pope went throughout Europe doing a brisk business. People were given the impression they could buy their way into heaven, even paying for sins yet to be committed—something clearly against church teaching.

The abuse of indulgences was one of the leading factors that led German monk Martin Luther to challenge the authority of the church. In October 1517 he nailed to the door of the church in Wittenburg his *Ninety-Five Theses*. This document, questioning the validity of several church practices, was the start of the Reformation.

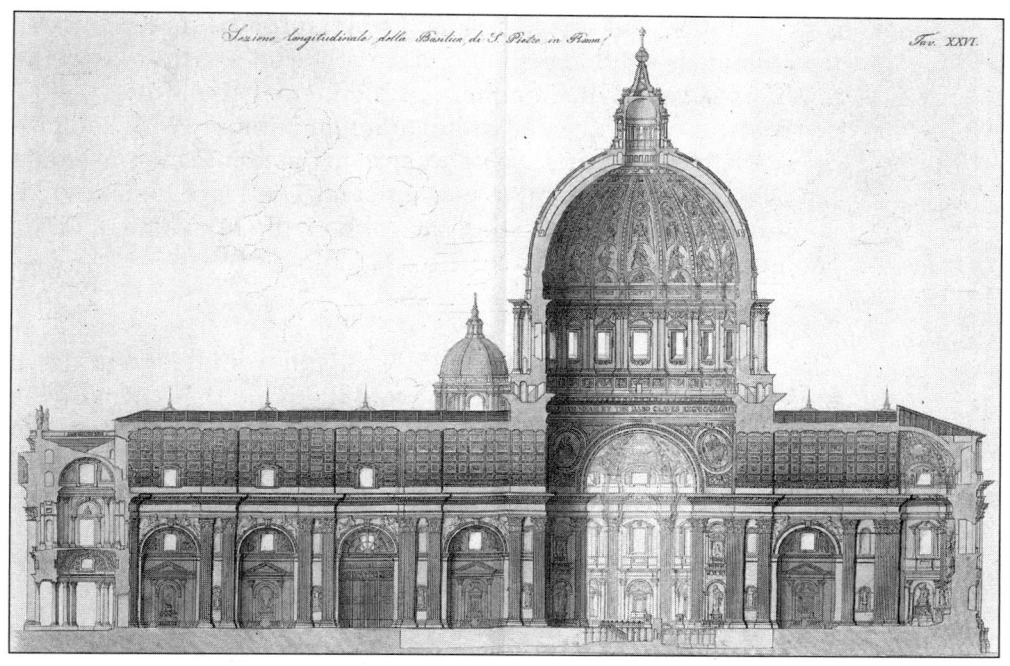

This cross section of St. Peter's Basilica shows the long arm of the nave and the large dome positioned over the altar. Original plans for the basilica called for a more geometrical design.

A BOLD PLAN

Bramante's plan was big and bold, covering almost 260,000 square feet, much more than the present-day church. He designed the church in the form of a Greek cross—a central square from which four arms extend equal lengths at right angles. The Greek cross, with its geometrical precision, was thought to be a symbol of the universality of Jesus and of Christianity.

Bramante's version was to have one huge hemispherical dome—much like that of the ancient Roman temple known as the Pantheon—over the high altar in the center and smaller domes over each arm of the cross. Two tall bell towers would stand on each side of the main entrance.

Where was the entrance to be? For twelve hundred years it had faced east, but Bramante—certainly no respecter of tradition—wanted to reorient the entire building to face south. His object was to have the church face the ancient Egyptian obelisk, or column, that had been part of Caligula's circus. To do so he would have to move Peter's tomb in order to keep it below the high altar. This was too much even for Julius, and Bramante was forced to keep the church orientation unchanged. To protect the sacred site of the tomb, he in fact built a temporary structure out of marble.

Bramante had to work within other limitations. Work had progressed on the western choir and apse to the point where it would have been uneconomical to tear it down. Therefore he had to incorporate the already existing sites of both the high altar, and the choir and apse to the west of the altar, into his plan.

"Knock It Down"

That did not mean, however, that Bramante could not tear down almost everything else. When he told the pope that virtually the entire Constantinian basilica would have to be destroyed to make room for the new building, Julius simply said, "Knock it down."[8] Bramante did not need to be told twice. He destroyed frescos, altars, mosaics, and statuary more than a thousand years old. So complete was the devastation that the Romans gave Bramante the name Il Ruinante, or "The Wrecker."

At last the day came—April 18, 1506—when construction on the new building officially began. A deep trench was dug at a point where one of the four tremendous piers that would hold up the dome would rise. Julius descended a ladder, clad in his white robes and three-tiered mitre, or crown, to lay the first stone—a block of white marble on which he had inscribed his intention to build the grandest church in Christendom. The solemn ceremony was cut short, however, when the number of people crowding around the trench threatened to cave it in. Julius hurriedly laid the stone—a little crookedly—and scrambled back up the ladder.

A year later the other three piers were dedicated and construction began. Slowly the immense structures—squares sixty feet each side—emerged from ground level and were built up to the cornices around the top. That is where they stayed. Julius died in 1513 and Bramante a year later.

Bramante's Impact

Even though he lived only long enough to see his plan barely begun, Bramante had an enormous impact on St. Peter's. Every architect who followed him had to take Bramante's Greek cross design into account. By spacing and building the four piers as he did, he had dictated the dimensions of both the interior and exterior, since any design would have to take into account the size of the central crossing and the size of the dome. Moreover those who succeeded Bramante considered him both divinely inspired, since his plan was blessed by the pope, and fully in keeping with the Renaissance feeling of breaking away from medieval forms.

Julius's successor, Pope Leo X, was very much in tune with the Renaissance but was much more interested in art than architecture. Just prior to Bramante's death, Leo recalled Giuliano da Sangallo and in 1514 appointed Giuliano, along with a talented monk named Fra Giocando and the artist Raphael, as architects of St. Peter's. Within two years both Giuliano and Fra Giocando had died, leaving Raphael in charge. One of his assistants, who was to figure prominently in later years, was Antonio da Sangallo, Giuliano's nephew.

BEST FOOT FORWARD

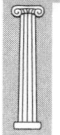

When architect Donato Bramante destroyed dozens of medieval artworks in demolishing the old St. Peter's to make way for a new basilica, there was at least one that was safe, even from Il Ruinante, or "The Wrecker." This was the bronze statue of Peter that sits in a place of honor in a niche of one of the four great pillars supporting the dome.

According to tradition the statue was originally that of the Roman god Jupiter but was converted into Peter's likeness by Pope Leo I in the 400s. Pope Gregory III is supposed to have placed it just to the northwest of Peter's shrine and to have begun the practice of having pilgrims kiss the outstretched toe of the saint's right foot.

Even Bramante would not have dared destroy such a revered symbol. It remained in the new St. Peter's but was moved to where it sits today, on a ledge about five feet from the floor. Hundreds of pilgrims file past each day, touching or kissing the toe, which has been rendered worn and shiny over the centuries.

Experts disagree on the origin of the statue. Some claim it is the work of Arnolfo di Cambio, a Roman sculptor of the 1200s. Others say that the bronze used in the statue is the same mix of lead and silver used in coins of the 600s. Still others say that both dates are correct, that di Cambio used bronze from an older statue and recast it, giving Peter a halo and keys symbolic of Jesus' kingdom.

Raphael's Plan

Raphael was a painter and thus uncomfortable with his role as chief architect. He did, however, draw up a new plan for St. Peter's. Bramante's piers were retained but the eastern arm of the Greek cross was lengthened and widened, thus transforming the design into a Latin cross, one in which one arm was much longer than the other three. This form of the cross is most usually associated with Christianity today.

Pope Leo highly regarded Raphael and his plan but lacked the money to make it a reality. Raphael died at age thirty-seven in 1520 before any work was accomplished. Leo appointed Baldas-

This painting shows (from left to right, center) Raphael, Bramante, and Michelangelo showing plans for St. Peter's Basilica to Pope Julius II.

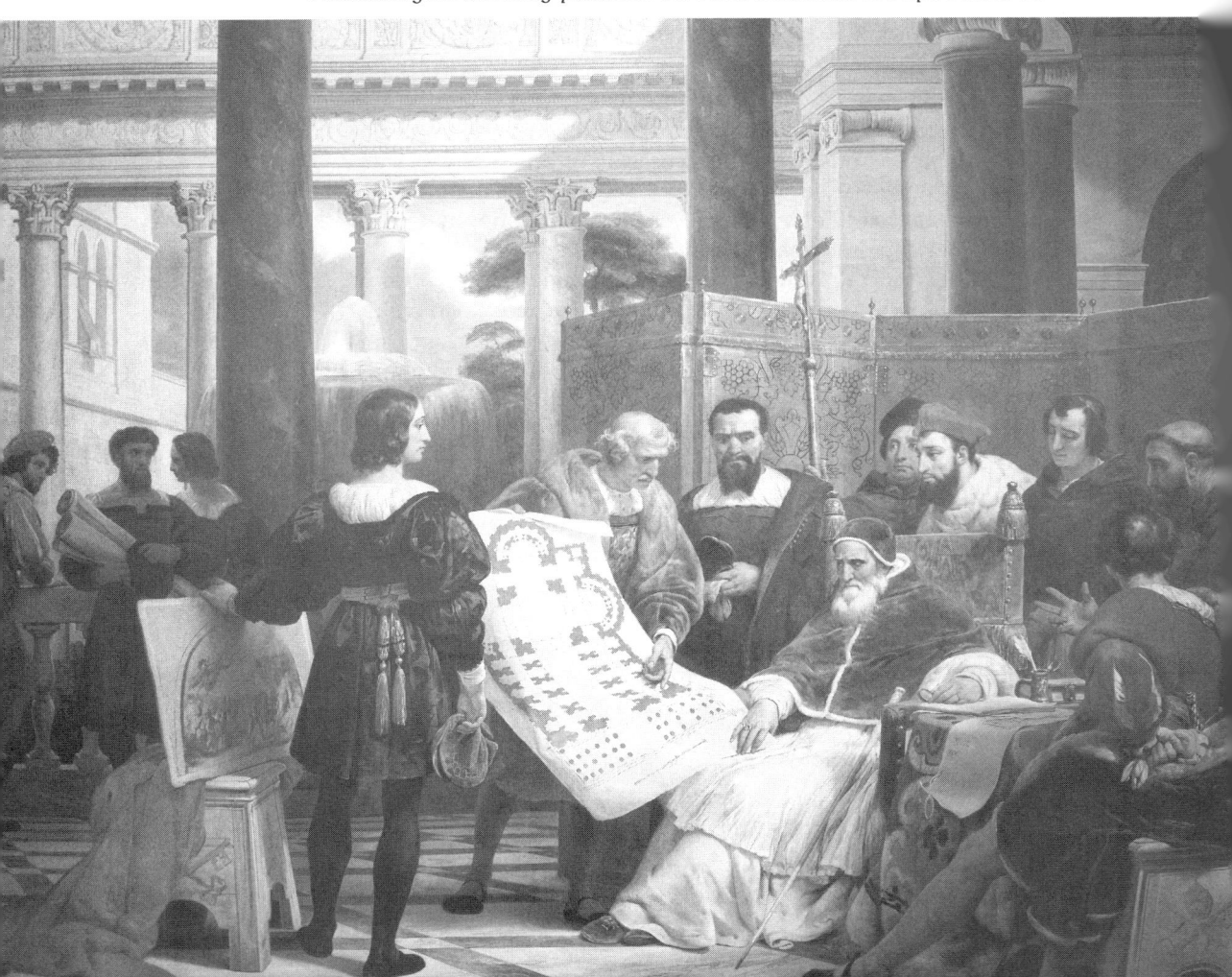

sare Peruzzi coarchitect with Antonio da Sangallo, but Peruzzi's design—going back to Bramante's Greek cross—likewise languished for lack of funds.

Leo's successor, Pope Adrian VI, accomplished little at the Vatican during his two-year reign. Neither did Adrian's successor, Pope Clement VII. Clement appointed Peruzzi chief architect and established a supervisory body, the Congregazione della Fabbrica di San Pietro, or Committee for the Building of St. Peter's, commonly known as the Fabbrica, which still oversees construction in the Vatican.

Clement, however, had problems far more serious than what to do about St. Peter's. The Protestant Reformation erupted in full force during his reign (1523–1534). England, the Scandinavian countries, and most of Germany left the Roman Catholic Church. Even worse, troops of the German Emperor Charles V invaded Italy in 1527, and Rome was brutally sacked. Priests and nuns were murdered; artworks smashed or ripped apart. Only Bramante's temporary housing kept the invaders from pillaging Peter's tomb. On Clement's death weeds and grass were growing within the cracks of the giant piers of St. Peter's.

ANTONIO DA SANGALLO

The next pope, Paul III, was determined to proceed with St. Peter's but had trouble keeping an architect. He first recalled Peruzzi, but he died in 1536 before work could begin. Paul then appointed Antonio da Sangallo, who dramatically altered Bramante's plan. He retained the four piers, having little choice, and also kept the southern, western, and northern arms of the Greek cross, but widened and lengthened the eastern arm thus—like Raphael before him—turning the building into a Latin cross. Unlike Raphael's plan, however, Sangallo's was crowded with pillars, chapels, and arcades.

Sangallo began work in 1538, aided by a group of relatives and close friends known by their enemies as *la setta Sangallesca,* or the Sangallo clique, and despised for diverting into their own pockets some of the funds intended for St. Peter's. Nevertheless Sangallo built a wall across the nave of the old church where the eastern end of his building would be and also raised the piers for the curved apses on the three short arms of the cross. He would have accomplished more but was diverted for four years by work in the palace. He died in 1546 shortly after resuming construction.

The pope tried two more architects: the first died before even arriving in Rome, the second absolutely refused to leave Venice. Paul then made an inspired decision, the most important one in the history of St. Peter's. He vowed that the next architect would be Michelangelo.

The great artist was now seventy-two years old. *The Last Judgment* was five years behind him; the Sistine Chapel thirty-one years. As usual Michelangelo protested. He was no architect, he told the pope. And, as usual, the pope had his way.

Michelangelo immediately ran into opposition from the Sangallo clique. Years before he had criticized Sangallo's design of a palace built for Paul before he was pope. Sangallo's clique never

Five years after completing The Last Judgment *(pictured) on the altar wall of the Sistine Chapel, and thirty-one years after completing the chapel's ceiling, Michelangelo was appointed architect for St. Peter's Basilica.*

MICHELANGELO DEFENDED

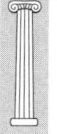

Michelangelo was stubborn and strong willed but found in Pope Julius II a pope just as unyielding. Once the artist fled from Rome rather than continue to work for the pope. He was finally convinced to meet the pope in the city of Bologna and knelt before Julius. The scene was described by a contemporary of the artist, Giorgio Vasari, in his *Lives of the Painters, Sculptors, and Architects:*

> He knelt before the pope, who looked wrathfully at him, and said as if in anger: "Instead of coming to us, you have waited for us to come and find you." Michelangelo spread his hands and humbly asked for pardon in a loud voice, saying he had acted in anger through being driven away, and that he hoped for forgiveness for his error. The bishop who presented him [Michelangelo] made excuses, saying that such men are ignorant of everything except their art. At this the pope waxed wroth [became angry], and striking the bishop with a mace he was holding, said: "It is you who are ignorant, to reproach him when we say nothing." The bishop therefore was hustled out by the attendants, and the pope's anger being appeased, he blessed Michelangelo.

forgot it. Thus, when Michelangelo suggested to the pope that Sangallo's Latin cross be abandoned for a Greek cross, the former architect's friends were incensed. They kept up a steady stream of complaints to the pope, accusing Michelangelo of everything from incompetence to theft, even though he had agreed to work without pay, "only for the love of God and in honour of the Apostle."[9]

MICHELANGELO'S PLAN

It was Michelangelo's genius that kept Pope Paul III and his three successors on his side. Whatever he might say against his accusers, his design said it more eloquently. He praised Bramante's design, perhaps as much to spite the *Sangallesca* as anything else, but made significant departures from it.

DESIGN PLANS FOR ST. PETER'S BASILICA

Bramante (1513)

Antonio da Sangallo (1539)

Michelangelo (1546 - 1564)

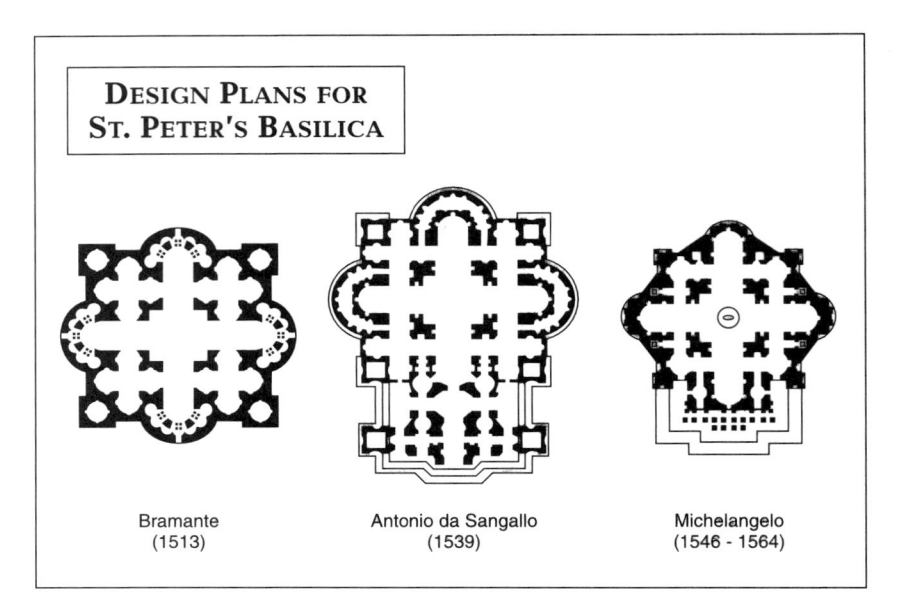

Michelangelo's plan was simpler and more elegant than Bramante's. The interior was less cluttered, with fewer chapels. He retained the central dome, with four smaller domes around it in a square, but the bell towers vanished. His greatest contribution, however, was to design windows to let in much more light than any of the previous designs.

Although he painted breathtaking frescos and designed elegant buildings, Michelangelo always maintained that he was only a sculptor. This was how he treated St. Peter's. J.S. Ackerman, an expert on Michelangelo's architecture, wrote that he considered buildings "organic forms capable of being molded and carved, of expressing movement, of forming symphonies of light, shadow and texture, like a statue."[10] He treated a building as a living thing in its own individual environment, a radical departure from the geometrical precision of Renaissance architecture.

In terms of square footage, Michelangelo's building was smaller (twenty-four thousand square feet) than Bramante's (thirty-five thousand), but it probably would have looked larger on the inside. Michelangelo's interior design was vertical, his use of unbroken space leading the viewer's eye up the columns built into the walls to the high, arched ceiling 150 feet above and the dome soaring up another three hundred feet. The arms of the Greek cross were 435 feet from one apse to the other.

Refusing to Quit

Michelangelo labored on St. Peter's eighteen years until his death in 1564. Despite the support of the popes, he was hounded all the while by the *Sangallesca*. At times he tried to resign, but at others steadfastly refused to be driven off, writing that if he left, "I should give satisfaction to sundry robbers here."[11]

When Michelangelo died St. Peter's was far from complete. The walls were in place on all but the east arm, and most of the ceiling had been finished. The cylindrical drum of the dome had been almost completed, but Michelangelo had been unable to decide finally on a design for what was to sit on it. The exterior was complete to the height of the interior walls, but the attic story had yet to be built.

Pope Julius II's will provided the drive to build the new St. Peter's after many years of stagnation. Bramante's determination cleared the way for construction and his talent gave the church its functional form. Michelangelo's genius transformed Bramante's functionality into a breathtaking work of art. Much had been accomplished, but the completion lay another seventy-five years in the future.

4

The Dome

Michelangelo was dead but, unlike many prior St. Peter's architects, his plan survived. Those who followed him followed closely his design for the basilica. So greatly was his memory treasured that neither popes nor architects dared to suggest any deviations. But when the body of the great church was finished, the great dome remained to be built. Michelangelo's immediate successors lacked the skill, the courage, or both, to undertake such a formidable task. It would require both an architect of great imagination and a pope of great determination.

Five months after Michelangelo's death, Pope Pius IV appointed Pirro Ligorio chief architect of St. Peter's and Jacopo Vignola his assistant. He gave both men strict orders not to deviate from Michelangelo's plan. When Pius IV was succeeded by Pius V in 1566, Ligorio attempted to make changes and was promptly dismissed.

Vignola, who stepped in as chief architect, had been an assistant to Michelangelo in 1551–1555. He faithfully carried out his former master's plan, including completion of the drum, until his own death in 1573, whereupon Pope Gregory XIII appointed Giacomo della Porta.

Della Porta greatly admired and was greatly influenced by Michelangelo but had ideas of his own. To put these ideas into practice he would have to wait for a like-minded pope. In the meantime he continued Michelangelo's plan for the main body of St. Peter's, which was largely completed under his direction.

Atop the building, however, there remained only the roofless drum completed by Vignola, waiting on the right combination of pope and architect to give it a dome worthy of the church. That pope was Sixtus V, whose reign of only five years (1585–1590) was yet to be among the most important of any pope except Julius II.

A Pope in a Hurry

Perhaps Pope Sixtus, sixty-five and in ill health when elected, thought he had only a short time to serve. Thus, when he began one of his many building projects, he urged his architects to use all possible speed in order that they might be completed before he died. So it was with St. Peter's. Sixtus was less dedicated to the memory of Michelangelo than he was determined the dome be finished during his papacy.

This fifteenth-century wooden model of St. Peter's dome, housed in the Vatican museums, was made prior to the actual dome's construction.

The papal treasury was almost empty when Sixtus was elected, but he soon filled it by increasing taxes, selling public offices, making loans at high interest, and cutting expenses everywhere except building. He paid his architects well and saw to it that work went quickly. In 1589 there were eight hundred men working round the clock.

Building such a large dome, however, took much more than mere manpower. In these centuries before reinforced concrete, large domes presented perhaps an architect's greatest challenge. At the time della Porta began, there were very few domes of comparable size in existence. One, the Pantheon, was right there in Rome. Built around A.D. 120 by the emperor Hadrian, its dome is 122 feet in diameter and 71 feet high. Experts still are not sure how the ancient builders achieved such a feat.

VIEW OF THE DOME

For centuries the only way to get a good view of the dome of St. Peter's was to climb a nearby hill or to look at it from a distance, such as from across the Tiber River. This state of affairs would not be changed until the twentieth century.

The dome was designed as a part of the Greek cross basilica of Bramante and Michelangelo and, had that design been retained, would have been visible in its entirety from the St. Peter's Square. The subsequent lengthening of the eastern nave, however, meant that those in the square would be able to see the curved upper part of the dome but not the drum underneath.

Moving further to the east would not have helped much. Just in front of St. Peter's Square was a maze of buildings and narrow streets known as the Borgo. All proposals to clear the area to the east of the square were strenuously opposed. The effect of St. Peter's, critics argued, according to English author Augustus Hare who is quoted in *St. Peter's* by James Lees-Milne, depended on "the sudden entrance into the sunlit piazza from the gloomy street."

It was the dictator Benito Mussolini who finally undertook the project, first suggested by Bramante, to tear down the buildings to the east and build a wide avenue leading to the square. The new street, the Via della Conciliazione, opened in 1937, thus affording a clear view of the dome to all who approached from the east.

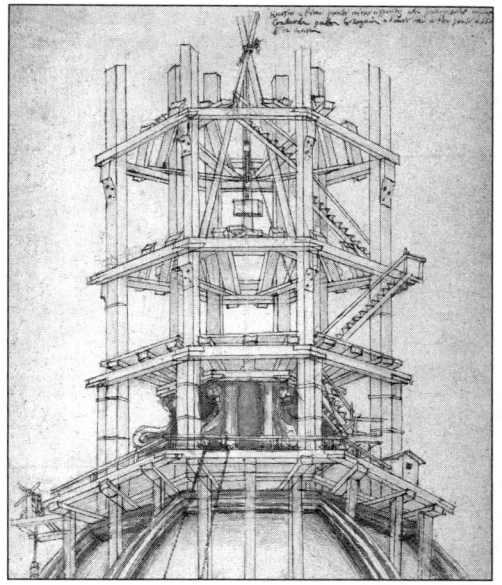

This drawing shows Brunelleschi's plans for the Duomo (left) and the magnificent end-result sitting atop the cathedral (right). The final plans for the dome of St. Peter's were based on the octagonal shape of the Duomo's dome.

THE DUOMO

Another, more recent dome, one Michelangelo had grown up with, rose above the Duomo, Florence's great cathedral. Completed in 1436 by Filippo Brunelleschi, it was one of the greatest engineering feats of the Renaissance.

The Pantheon's dome is an almost perfect hemisphere. That of the Duomo is an irregular octagon. Architectural historians have argued for centuries as to what Michelangelo's final design for St. Peter's dome was—if, indeed, he ever reached a decision.

Barely a year after his appointment as architect of St. Peter's, Michelangelo wrote to Florence for exact measurements of Brunelleschi's dome. Early drawings show that he was considering the same type of structure, more pointed than hemispherical. About 1560, however, he constructed a model in which the dome was more of a hemisphere.

Which type of dome would Michelangelo have built had he lived long enough? No one can tell. The great master was constantly changing his mind, sometimes well after construction began. His last indication, however, was the model with a hemispherical dome.

BRUNELLESCHI'S INFLUENCE

When Michelangelo began to design the dome of St. Peter's, he had two outstanding examples to draw from. The first was the Pantheon in Rome, built in the second century by the emperor Hadrian. The other was one Michelangelo had grown up with in Florence, the great dome of the Duomo, Florence's cathedral.

The Duomo dome was the work of Florentine architect, Filippo Brunelleschi, who lived from 1377 to 1446. He was one of the few architects who understood the importance of perspective. Painters of the early Renaissance had discovered the method of making lines in a drawing seem to come together, giving an idea of depth. Brunelleschi applied the concept to buildings, making liberal use of geometric principles.

In addition to being a work of art, however, the Duomo dome is an engineering masterpiece. Brunelleschi hit on the idea of a dome within a dome. The inner dome, more than six feet thick, provides the strength. An ingenious system of trusses from the inner dome helps support the outer dome.

There is little doubt Michelangelo had Brunelleschi's dome in mind when working on St. Peter's. As told in *The World of Michelangelo* by Robert Coughlan, someone once asked the architect/artist if he could build a dome for St. Peter's bigger than Brunelleschi's. "Bigger, yes," Michelangelo replied, "but not more beautiful."

Della Porta did not agree. He thought that a hemisphere would be too squat and rounded, out of keeping with the vertical lines of the main building. His problem was how to suggest changes in the great Michelangelo's plan without offending his memory. He told Pope Sixtus that he was afraid to complete the dome according to Michelangelo's plan because the thrust—the outward, horizontal pressure of the sides of the dome—would be too great and that it would collapse. A more vertical, oval shape, he said, would be far better. The weight of the dome would be more vertical than horizontal and would be easily absorbed by the great piers.

A Dramatic Display

The architect hit on a dramatic way to display his design to the pope. Invited by Pope Sixtus to show him a drawing of the new design, della Porta decided to make the drawing full size. He fastened hundreds of sheets of paper together and made the drawing as large as the dome itself would be.

The only way he could display such a huge drawing and ensure safety from wind or weather was to spread it on the floor of the nave of the Church of St. Paul's Outside the Walls, the largest covered space in Rome. Sixtus viewed the gigantic layout from the highest balcony available and was so impressed that he approved the design on the spot.

There was little wonder that the pope wasted no time in making his decision. He wanted the dome finished in his lifetime, no matter what the cost. As a result construction took only twenty-two months—lightning speed compared to the snail's pace at which other building at St. Peter's had occurred.

The dome designed by della Porta is more oval than rounded. In profile it is much like the dome of the United States Capitol in Washington, D.C., one of many buildings in the world that have been inspired by St. Peter's. The other changes were subtle and relatively unimportant. Ornamental lion masks were added around the top of the drum, since the lion was the symbol of Sixtus's family. The shape of some windows were altered, and the ribs running from the top to the bottom of the dome were narrowed.

THE LANTERN

The only other important change by della Porta was to reduce the height of the lantern, the cylindrical structure on top of the dome circled with windows and surmounted by a cross. Michelangelo's taller version might have been appropriate for a rounded dome and might have been a more prominent feature than the dome beneath it. Della Porta's much taller dome, however, needed a proportionally shorter lantern.

Della Porta's changes to Michelangelo's dome design were only to the exterior. He agreed that Michelangelo's hemispherical design was best for the interior. He was able to bring this about because there are actually two domes—the heavy stone exterior and the much lighter interior shell inside it. Such an arrangement, besides allowing for the different shapes of the dome, is extremely practical. By climbing a staircase on the outer surface of the interior dome, workers can more easily reach and make repairs to both domes. The space between the two domes also helps prevent dampness from seeping through to the interior.

The interior of the dome, indeed, deserves to be protected. Sunlight streams in from windows in the drum and lantern. Running around the drum in Latin, in letters six feet high, are Jesus' words to Peter, giving him the keys to the kingdom and making him, in the eyes of the Roman Catholic Church, Jesus' representative on earth. Above each pillar are four gigantic depictions of the four Evangelists—Matthew, Mark, Luke, and John—huge mosaics created with thousands of pieces of colored stone.

INSIDE THE DOME

The walls of the dome are divided into sixteen sections, each covered with representations of popes, saints, and angels. Just below the lantern is another inscription, this one dedicated to St. Peter

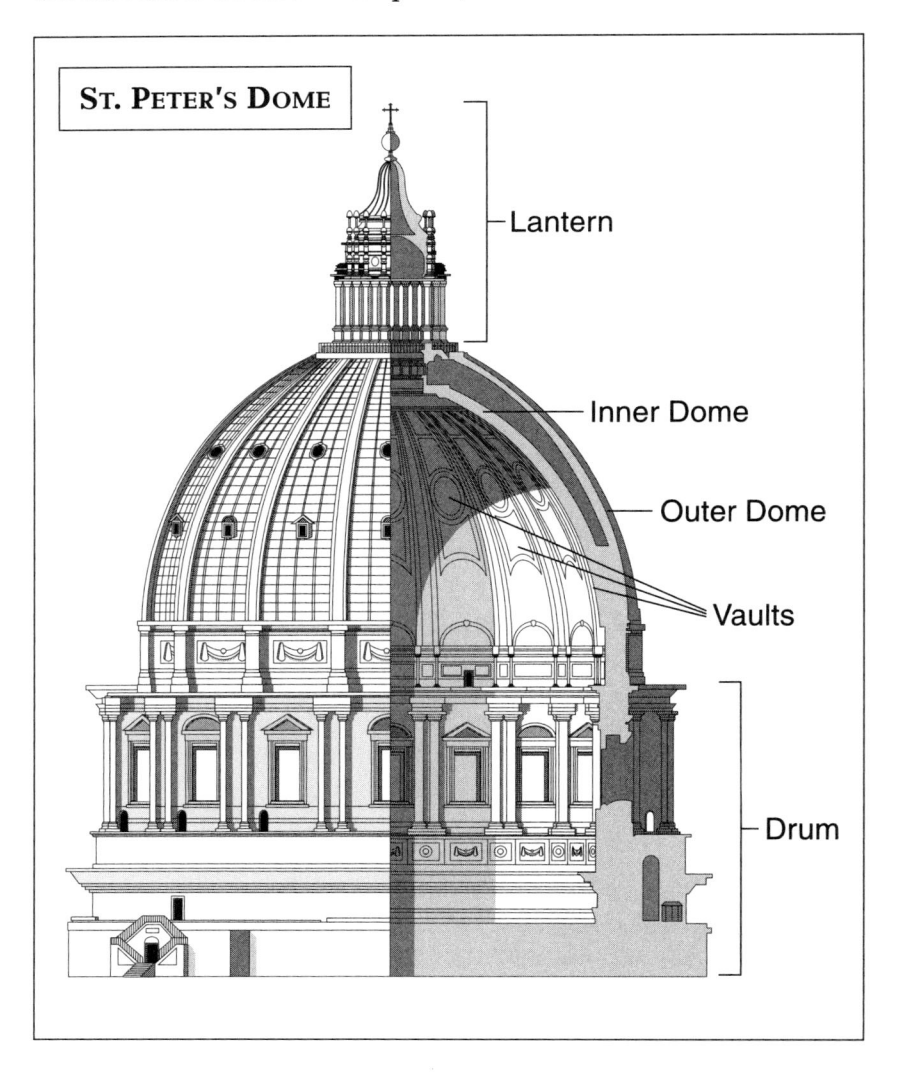

ST. PETER'S DOME

- Lantern
- Inner Dome
- Outer Dome
- Vaults
- Drum

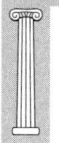

> **THE *SAMPIETRINI***
>
> The lantern on the dome of St. Peter's stands more than 450 feet above the floor of the basilica. Through its windows tourists by the thousands gaze on the metropolis of Rome spread below. Who cleans those windows from the outside? For that matter, who gains access to the tops of gigantic columns to hang the large banners used for special ceremonies? Who keeps the hundreds of statues and monuments free of the grime of a modern city? The men charged with this responsibility are the Sampietrini, a small army of workers whose lives and careers are dedicated to the maintenance of the basilica.
>
> In 1600 a mason named Zabagila working on the basilica suggested to the Congregazione della Fabbrica, the body overseeing all work done there, that St. Peter's was too precious to be trusted to casual laborers hired for a week or a month do to this or that job. He proposed a permanent workforce, one that would devote all the skills of its members to St. Peter's.
>
> The overseers agreed and Zabagila recruited thirty young men to be trained in all the crafts necessary to maintain St. Peter's. These original Sampietrini eventually brought their sons into the company, and membership became, for the most part, hereditary.
>
> Today's *Sampietrini* are seldom seen by the public, but the result of their work is seen everywhere. Among them are not only plumbers, electricians, and carpenters, but also glaziers, painters, plasterers, and artists to keep fresh the treasures of centuries.

and bearing the name of Pope Sixtus and the year 1590. Finally, painted on the ceiling of the lantern, is God emerging from the clouds to look down on those far below.

The dome, like much of the interior of St. Peter's, is so well proportioned that visitors, although realizing they are standing in a very large building, have difficulty grasping how large it actually is. Three space shuttles could be stacked end to end and still stand short of the top by about one hundred feet.

The decoration of the dome's interior, however, had to wait for another pope. Sixtus lived only long enough to see the dome completed. A year after he died in 1690, the lantern was installed and the cross placed on top, 450 feet above the pavement.

Sixtus did remain on the throne long enough to see another project completed. His predecessors had often expressed the wish that the Egyptian obelisk to the south of the basilica could be moved and made part of the overall plan. The obelisk, an eighty-three-foot column of solid granite, was constructed in 1583 B.C. and brought to Rome as a trophy by the emperor Caligula in A.D. 37. Caligula placed it in his circus, probably on the north wall, where it remained until Sixtus decided to move it.

PLENTY OF PROPOSALS

In 1585 the pope had a full-sized wooden version of the obelisk erected in the plaza. He liked what he saw and called for proposals to move the real one. Many thought this engineering feat impossible. Even Michelangelo had thought so. Yet five hundred architects and mathematicians were reported to have suggested to Pope Sixtus how it might be done. Some went so far as to suggest magic or prayer. Sixtus wasted little time on such far-fetched ideas but paid more attention to a model proposed by Domenico Fontana, della Porta's chief assistant.

A model crane was constructed only of light wood, but an ingenious system of windlasses, or winches, was able to lift a model obelisk made of lead. Sixtus, always one for quick decisions, approved the plan without further ado.

While outwardly confident, Fontana had grave doubts about his own scheme. No one had ever built a machine capable of lifting such an enormous weight, estimated at a million pounds. The architect privately told friends that he might fail. Just in case he did, he had a fast horse ready for an escape from Rome and the pope's wrath.

By April 30, 1586, the obelisk had been surrounded by the crane and secured with iron bands and dozens of ropes. The earth around the base had been removed. One hundred and forty large horses and eight hundred men waited to pull on the ropes. After an open-air mass, Fontana moved into position atop a rostrum. Hundreds of spectators looked on from surrounding windows and balconies.

When Fontana gave the signal, the men strained at the ropes. Others whipped the horses into motion. The huge obelisk jerked, then rose slowly into the air. The crowd cheered and the workers paraded around the plaza, Fontana riding on their shoulders.

RAISING THE OBELISK

In May the obelisk was gently lowered to a horizontal position on rollers and moved to its new home directly in front of the east side of St. Peter's. There it sat until Pope Sixtus chose the most auspicious day for the next step. He picked September 14. It was a Wednesday—considered his lucky day—and also the day of the Feast of the Exaltation of the Cross.

Again Fontana and his army of workers received the pope's blessing then moved into place. An even greater crowd than before watched. Fontana rang a bell, and horses and men began to pull.

Sixtus had called for absolute quiet so that all workers could hear Fontana's signals. Anyone making noise, he vowed, would be executed, and he had a gallows put up in the plaza to show he meant business. According to legend, a sailor from the town of Bordighera saw some of the ropes begin to smoke from the friction

Many fanciful ideas were considered for moving the Vatican's obelisk, including divine intervention by cherubs and angels (left). Ultimately the obelisk was gently lowered with rollers and moved to the plaza (right).

they were undergoing and cried, "Water them!" He was arrested, but pardoned by Sixtus, who granted his wish that Bordighera supply palm leaves to St. Peter's for Palm Sunday services in the future. Whether the story is true or not, the town did, indeed, supply palms for many years.

In 1586 Roman citizens celebrated when the Vatican's Egyptian obelisk was transported and finally brought to rest in St. Peter's Square, where it stands today.

Eventually the obelisk was raised to vertical and gently lowered onto the base that had been built to receive it. When it was in place and the ropes removed, Rome erupted in celebration. The people of the time saw the moving of the obelisk as much more than a feat of engineering. It was if Christianity had, after many centuries, at last won out over the paganism—Egyptian and ancient Roman—embodied in the obelisk. The monument had been an enduring symbol of the dreadful persecutions of the early Christians. Now, moved to the front of the church honoring the greatest martyr of them all, surmounted by a cross, it represented the triumph of Christianity.

Not all the construction at St. Peter's during the late 1500s dealt with towering domes and tall monuments, however. With the central portion of the church nearing completion, the most sacred part of the basilica, the altar over the site of Peter's tomb, drew some attention. Pope Clement VIII ordered the ancient apse of the Constantinian church to be demolished and Bramante's protective covering of the high altar removed.

THE NEW ALTAR

The altar itself, a smallish affair built in the 1100s, was considered insufficient. Della Porta replaced it with a huge table fashioned from a single piece of white marble. Clement celebrated the first mass at the new altar in 1594 and, from then to now, only the pope is allowed to do so.

Della Porta then went below the surface, digging out a horseshoe-shaped space directly underneath the altar. The space provided access to the marble covering built during Constantine's time to enclose, according to tradition, the still more ancient marker of St. Peter's grave. A concave opening in the marble wall is called the Niche of the Pallia. Here, the night before a new archbishop is consecrated by the pope, his pallium, or stole of office, rests directly above the site of Peter's tomb.

The dome was finished. The obelisk was moved. The new altar had been consecrated. And yet St. Peter's was still a work in progress. Much work remained on the main body of the church, especially the eastern arm. It would be here that the builders of St. Peter's would dramatically depart from Michelangelo's design.

The Latin Cross

While St. Peter's dome was being completed in less than two years, work on the main body of the building proceeded at its usual leisurely pace. Eventually, however, popes and architects reached a point, the end of the eastern arm or front of the church, where their decisions would determine the basilica's final shape and exterior appearance. Even the memory of the great Michelangelo would not be enough to save his Greek cross design.

After della Porta died in 1602, work on St. Peter's came almost to a standstill for three years. Carlo Maderno, who had been an assistant to della Porta, was appointed chief architect by Pope Clement VIII but contented himself with putting the finishing touches on the south, west, and north arms of the cross.

Clement, meanwhile, reorganized the Congregazione della Fabbrica. This oversight body, formerly made up of representative from throughout Europe, became much more Italian in character, dominated by local cardinals and led by the cardinal whose duties included being chief priest of St. Peter's. This organization has lasted, with only minor adjustments, to the present time.

No sooner had the new Fabbrica been formed than it had to deal with the size and style of the nave, the eastern arm of the cross. Despite Pope Julius II's instructions to Bramante to knock the old basilica down, a considerable portion remained on the east end, separated from the new church by the wall erected in 1538. As work on the new church plodded along decade after decade, the pope and his priests still held services in the chapels of the older one.

Sign from Above

The twelve-hundred-year-old structure, however, was getting ever more rickety. In 1605 a storm broke when a service was being conducted in one of the chapels. A huge clap of thunder shook the building to the point where a large block of marble crashed to the ground next to the altar. No one was hurt but the Fabbrica decided that every part of the Constantinian basilica still standing had to come down.

There was no wholesale destruction of artistic and religious treasures as there had been under Bramante. The Vatican archivist carefully cataloged ancient monuments as they were either placed in storage or moved to the new building. Relics of saints—a finger bone here, a lock of hair there—were moved to safety. The tombs of popes dead for centuries were opened and their moldering remains reverently interred elsewhere.

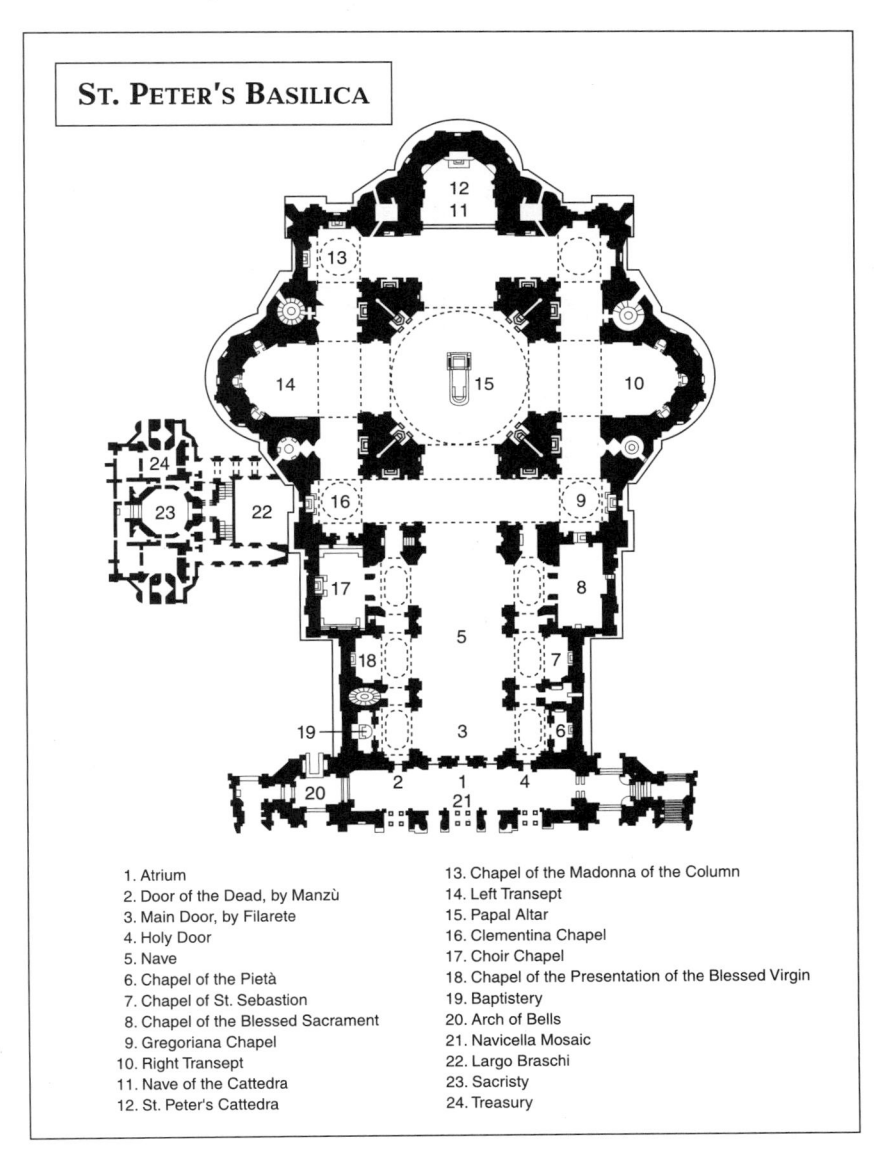

ST. PETER'S BASILICA

1. Atrium
2. Door of the Dead, by Manzù
3. Main Door, by Filarete
4. Holy Door
5. Nave
6. Chapel of the Pietà
7. Chapel of St. Sebastion
8. Chapel of the Blessed Sacrament
9. Gregoriana Chapel
10. Right Transept
11. Nave of the Cattedra
12. St. Peter's Cattedra
13. Chapel of the Madonna of the Column
14. Left Transept
15. Papal Altar
16. Clementina Chapel
17. Choir Chapel
18. Chapel of the Presentation of the Blessed Virgin
19. Baptistery
20. Arch of Bells
21. Navicella Mosaic
22. Largo Braschi
23. Sacristy
24. Treasury

This sixteenth-century painting depicts a coronation while construction of St. Peter's dome takes place in the background. It was during the sixteenth and seventeenth centuries that St. Peter's took on its modern-day appearance.

When all the precious objects had been moved, the ancient chapels were unconsecrated, taking away their status as holy places. Crosses and other religious symbols were removed. Altars were taken down. Finally only the bare walls remained—but not for long.

On February 18, 1606 workers began demolition. They started with the roof, taking down the marble cross erected by Constantine so many centuries ago. Ironically they found a name carved in Greek on the base—Agrippina, mother of the emperor Nero who had crucified Peter.

By March the walls began to come down. Two huge, black marble columns from Africa were saved for reuse in the new building, but most everything else was carted away. On November 15, the last service was conducted in Rossellino's old choir before it, too, fell before the workers' pickaxes. The remains of two of the Vatican's most influential popes, Sixtus IV and Julius II, uncle and nephew, were removed from their separate tombs and buried side by side.

NEW TIMES, NEW STYLES

As the old basilica was coming down, the pope and Fabbrica were trying to determine what would go up in its place. The

St. Peter's Basilica from the Tiber River.

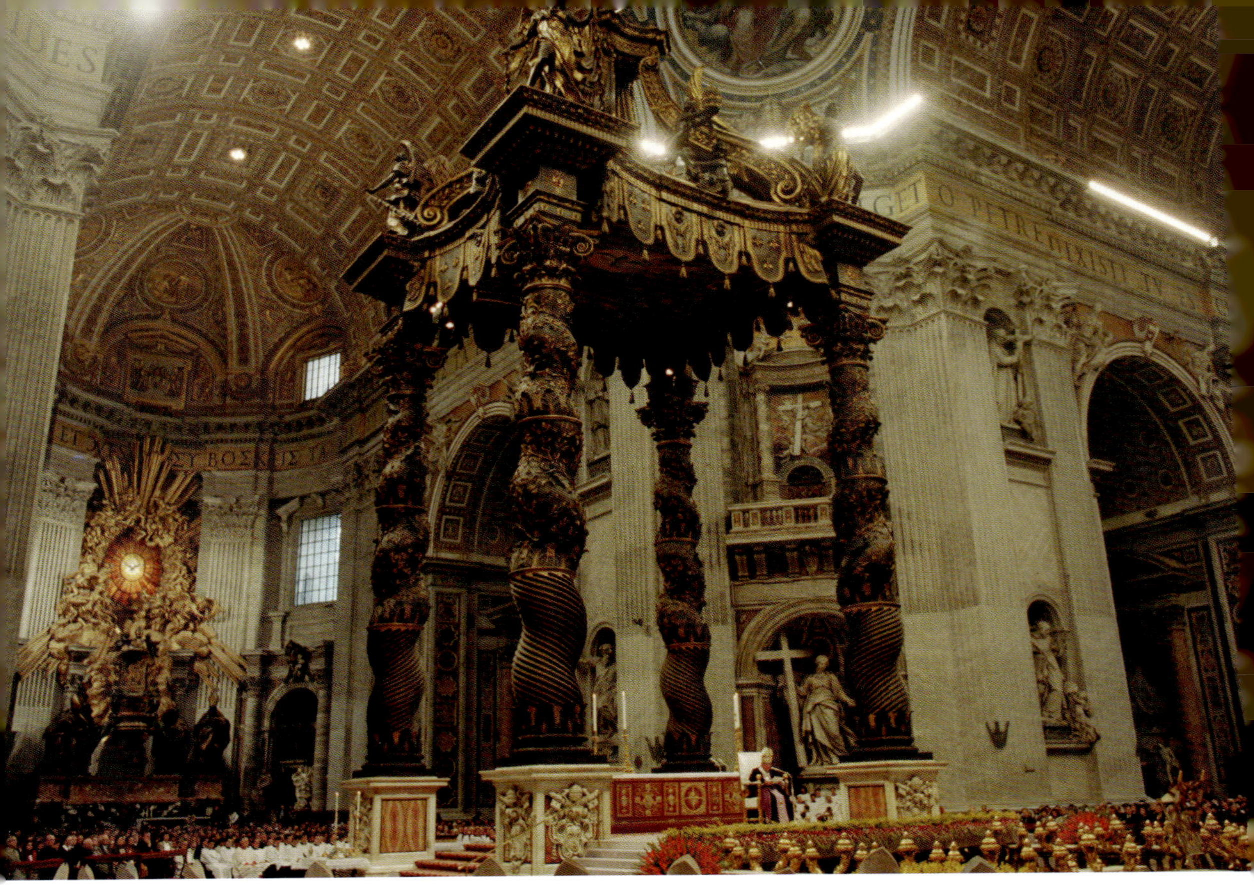

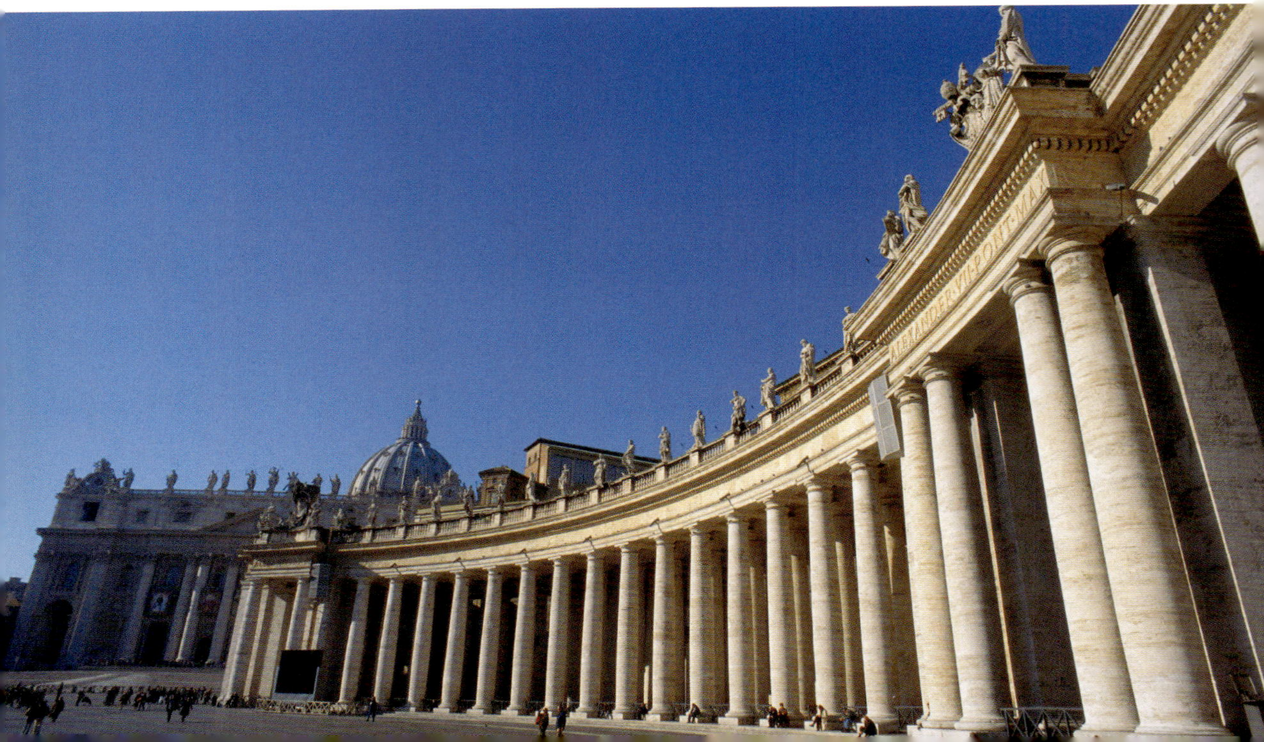

The interior of St. Peter's Basilica (top left), highlighting the cattedra Petri, *or Throne of Peter (left, in photo), and Bernini's* baldacchino *(center, in photo), Bernini's colonnade in St. Peter's Square, (bottom left), and a statue of Pope Pius IX on the facade of St. Peter's Basilica.*

The Erithraean Sibyl, *(1508-1512) by Michelangelo, detail of the Sistine Chapel.*

The Delphic Sibyl, *(1508-1512) by Michelangelo, detail of the Sistine Chapel.*

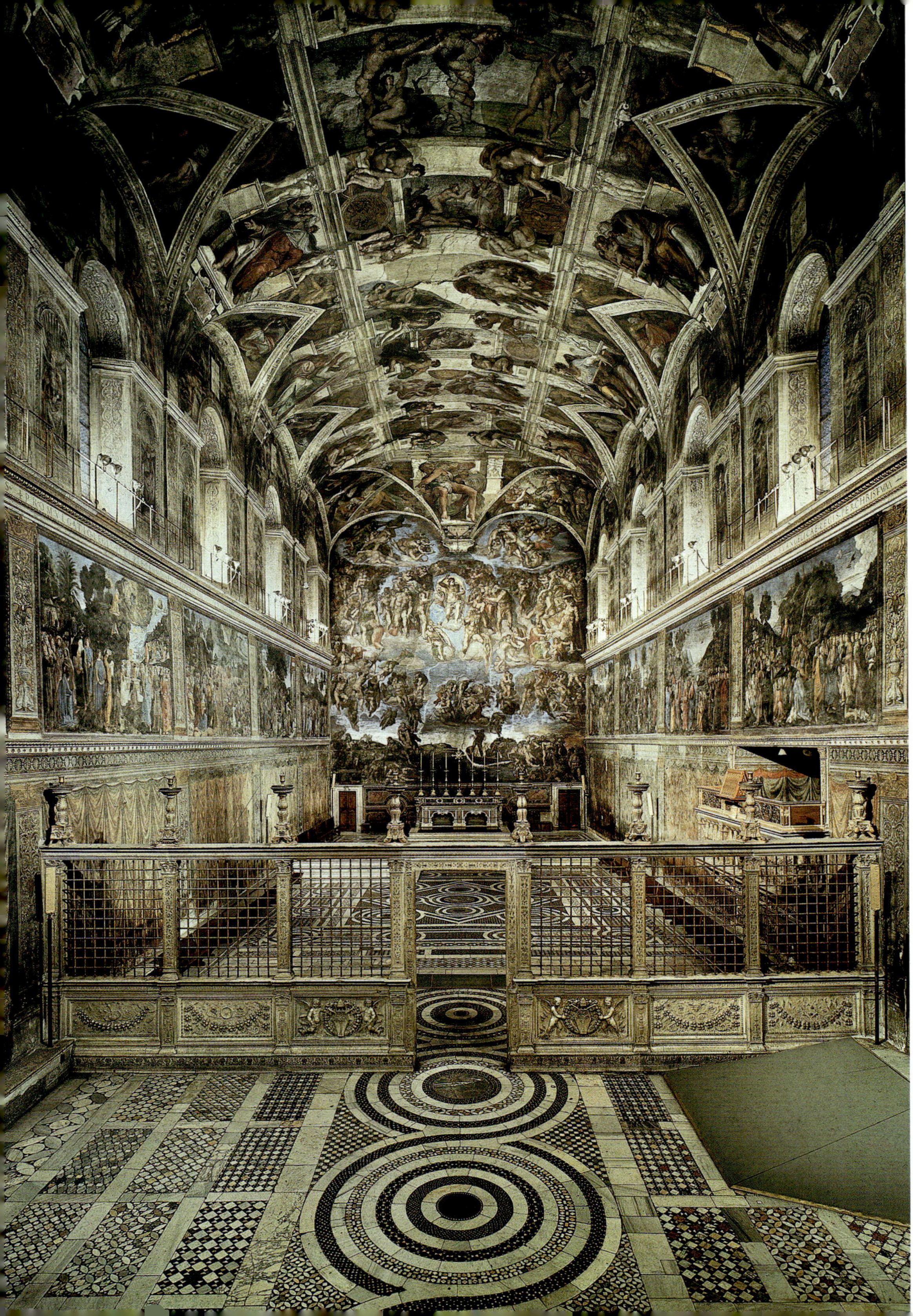

Interior view of the Sistine Chapel (left). Detail of God from the Creation of Stars and Planets, *(top), and the* Creation of Adam, *(bottom), (1508-1512) by Michelangelo, detail of the Sistine Chapel.*

The Pietà, (1499) by Michelangelo.

The Laocoön Group, (first century) Roman copy by an unknown artist.

View of the interior of the dome of St. Peter's Basilica (above). Moses' Journey to Egypt, (fifteenth century) by Pietro Perugino (top, right). St. Nicholas and the Tempest, (1425) detail from the Quaratesi polyptych, by Gentile da Fabriano (bottom, right).

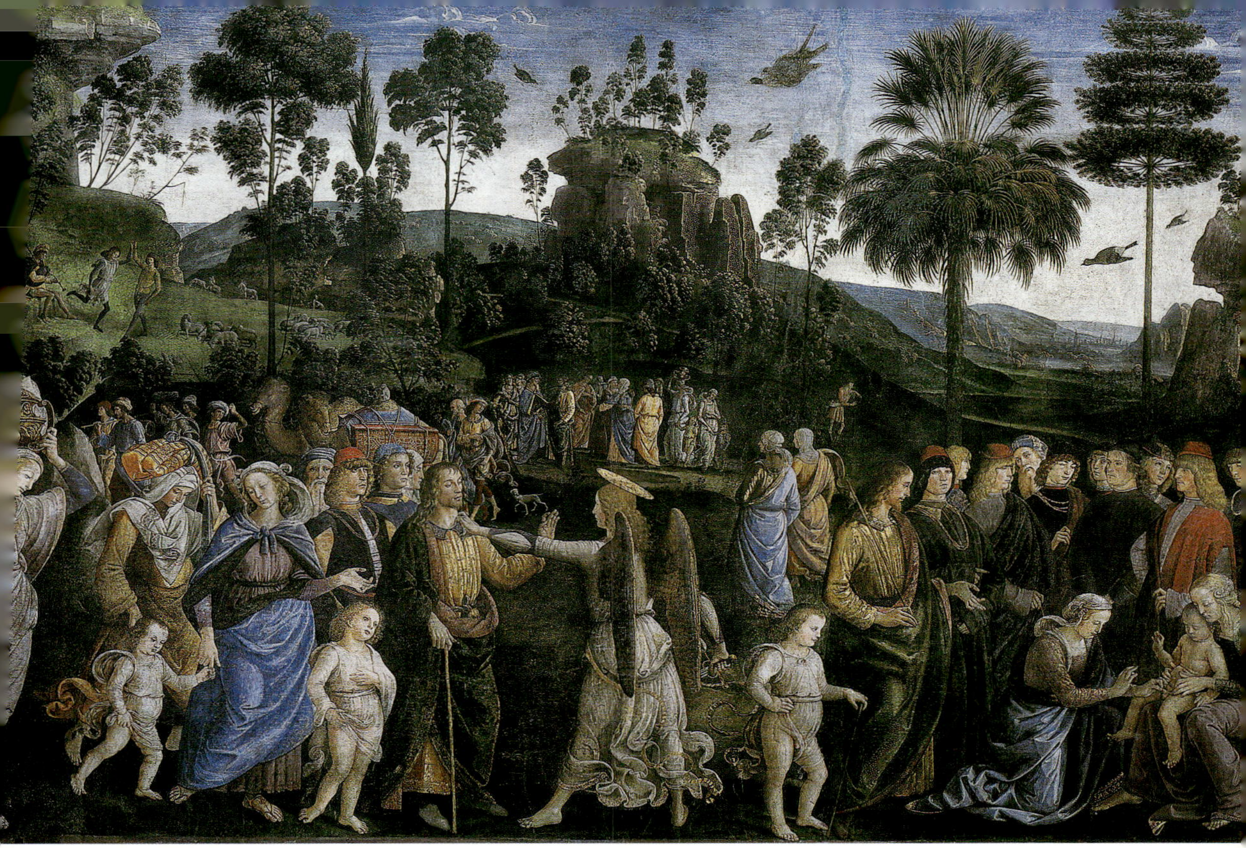

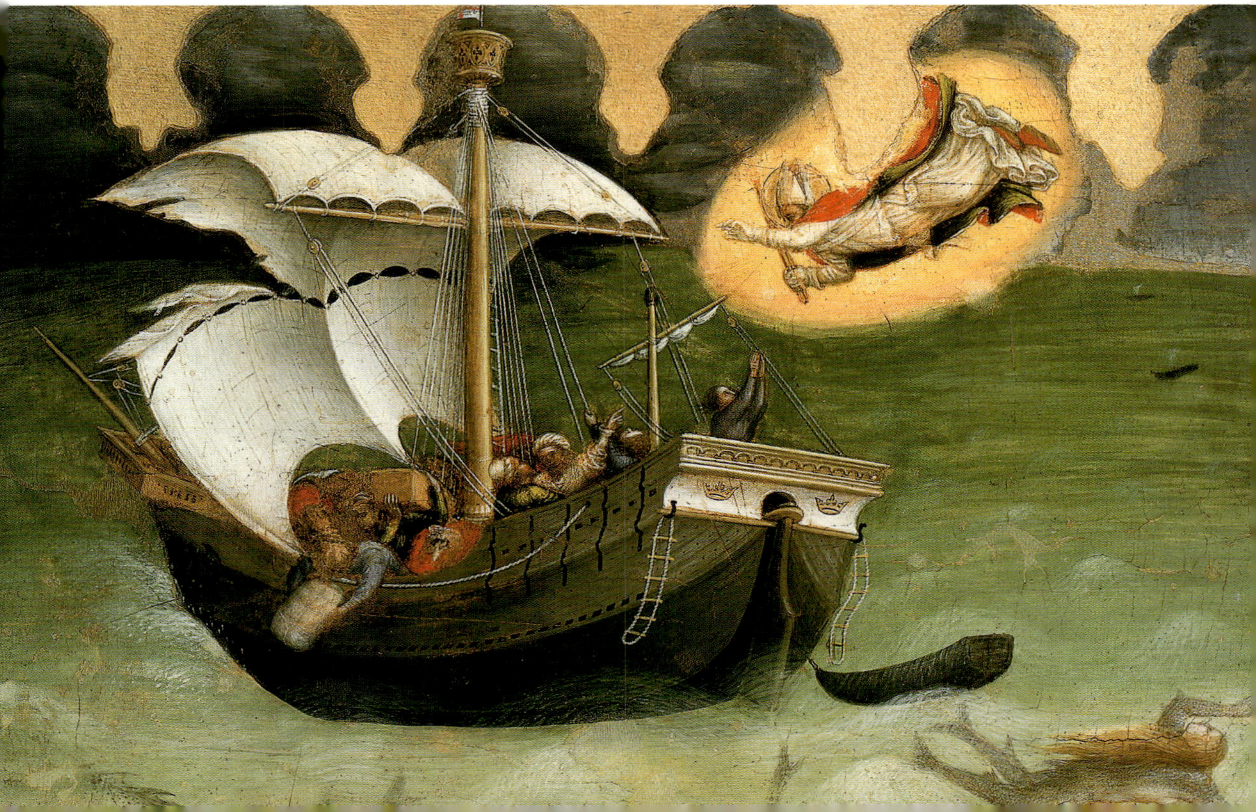

Rest on the Flight into Egypt, *(1573)* by Federico Barocci *(above)*. Madonna and Child with St. John the Baptist, *(fifteenth century)* by the Umbrian School *(right)*.

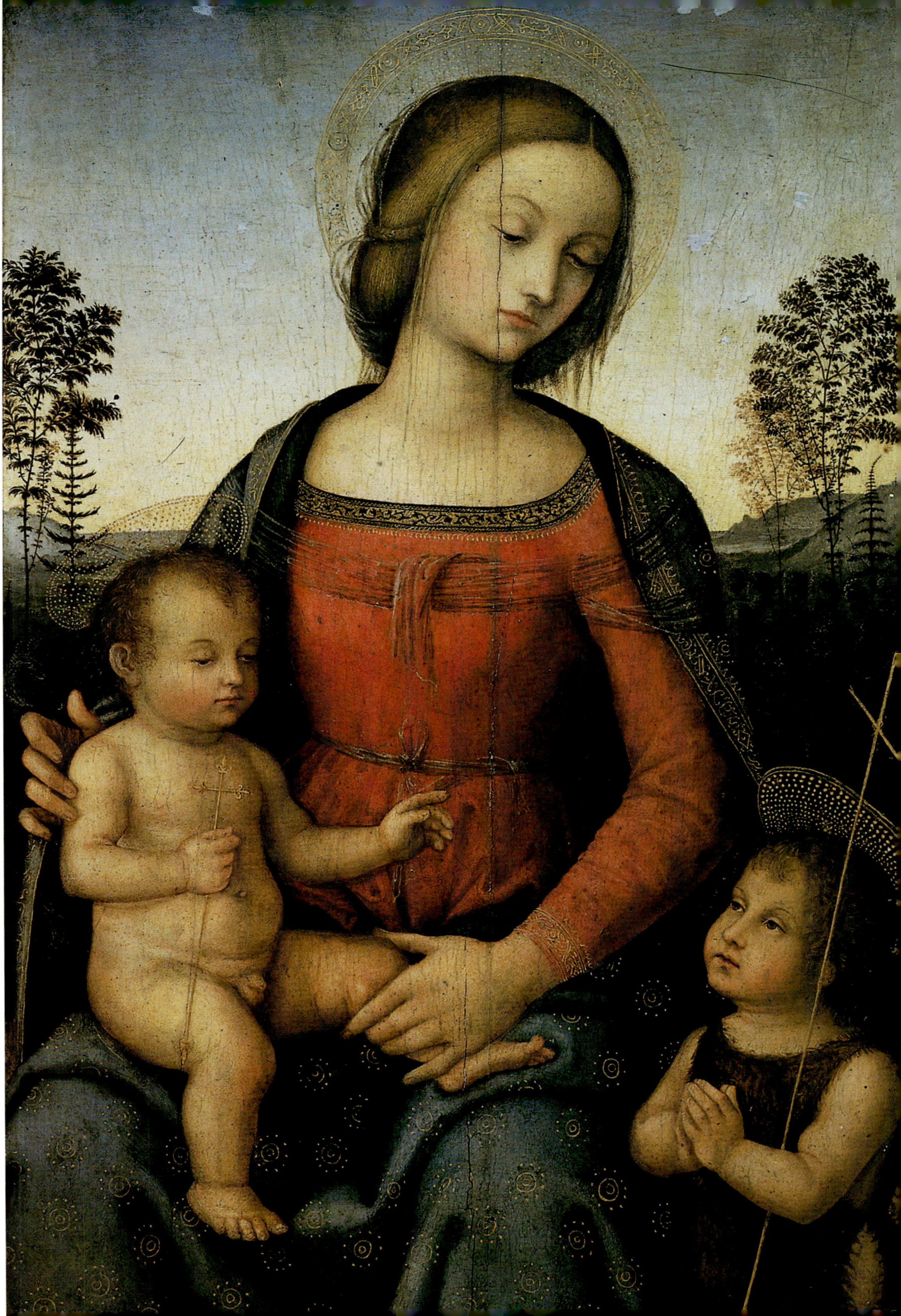

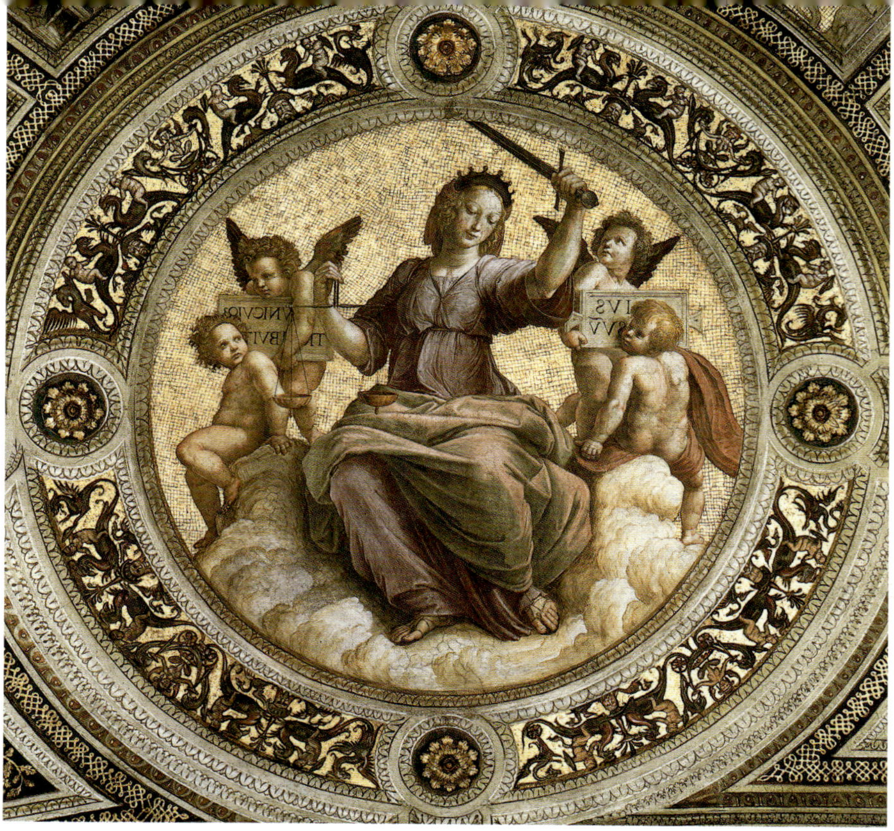

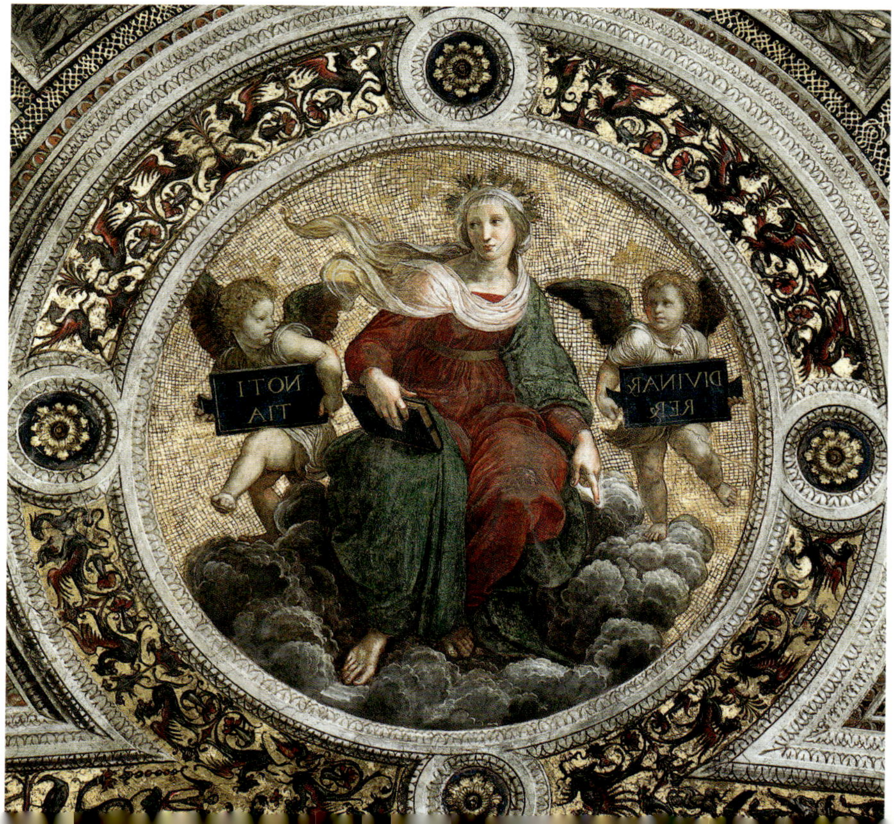
NOTI
TIA

Detail of Justice (top, left), and Allegory of Theology (bottom, left), from the ceiling of the Stanza della Signatura, (fifteenth century) by Raphael. A Swiss Guard (above).

Saint Jerome, *(1480) by Leonardo da Vinci.*

Greek cross of Bramante and Michelangelo had been considered the ideal design, but times had changed. The geometric precision so valued by Renaissance architects had given way to more expressive styles—mannerism with its deliberate distortions and exaggerations, and baroque with its emotional appeal and prolific decoration. The Greek cross might be mathematically precise, but it did not convey the same emotion as the Latin cross, the type Jesus is most depicted to have been crucified upon.

There was a practical aspect to the Latin cross as well. The papal processions on great religious holidays had grown far longer than the nave. It simply was not long enough to accommodate all the cardinals, archbishops, bishops, and abbots, let alone the various court officials, ordinary priests, and altar boys.

In 1607 Pope Paul V convened a group of ten prominent architects, Maderno among them. They recommended the nave be lengthened to form a Latin cross. The curia—a court made up of

Pope Paul V (pictured) commissioned a group of ten architects led by Carlo Maderno to finalize plans for St. Peter's Basilica in 1607.

cardinals—agreed, and Maderno was given the task of designing the new structure.

Whether Maderno supported the Latin cross plan is unclear. He was criticized during his lifetime and has been ever since for departing from Michelangelo's design. In 1613 he wrote, perhaps in self-defense, that the pope and cardinals had forced him to execute a plan he did not really approve of.

Maderno's Design

Regardless, Maderno undertook the design. Michelangelo had designed two bays, or recessed areas, on either side of the nave. In each bay was a chapel—the Clementine Chapel to the south and the Gregorian Chapel to the north. Maderno extended the nave by three more bays on each side. The two westernmost bays are approximately the same size as Michelangelo's and house the Choir Chapel and Blessed Sacrament Chapel.

THE PIETÀ

Michelangelo's *Pietà* is one of the most famous statues in the world. Practically the first thing one sees on entering St. Peter's is a huge throng to the right clustered around one of the bays in Maderno's nave. The crowd is gazing at the *Pietà*.

Yet when it first went on view, admirers were not sure who had carved it. Giorgio Vasari, who wrote a study of the lives of Renaissance artists, told the story that Michelangelo overheard people discussing who among the more famous sculptors of the day might have done this great work. Late that night, Vasari wrote, Michelangelo bribed an attendant to let him into the chapel where the statue stood. He took a small chisel and hammer and carved in Latin on the band across Mary's chest, "Michelangelo Buonarroti of Florence made this." It was the only work he ever signed.

The *Pietà* is best seen from close up at eye level. Sadly, that is no longer possible. In 1972 a mentally disturbed man jumped across a barrier and smashed Mary's arm and face with a hammer. The statue has since been restored, but now must be seen on an elevated platform behind a thick sheet of protective glass.

The other two bays on each side are more shallow and contain tombs and monuments. In the southeast corner is the Baptistery, the font of which is covered by a highly polished stone lid that had once covered the sarcophagus, or coffin, of the emperor Hadrian who died in A.D. 138.

The northeast corner, however, is the part of St. Peter's that attracts more tourists than any other. Here, set behind a protective sheet of heavy glass, is one of the most famous statues in the world, Michelangelo's *Pietà*. Showing the Virgin Mary holding the crucified Jesus in her lap, the *Pietà* was carved by Michelangelo when he was only twenty-five years old and made him famous throughout Italy.

On 8 March 1607 work began on the foundations. Two months later the first stone, having been blessed by the pope, was put into place. Seven hundred workers labored for eight years and by Palm Sunday, of 1615, the wall dividing the two parts of the nave was demolished.

Size of St. Peter's

Maderno's design had increased the length of the nave by more than a third to 726 feet, more than two entire football fields longer. By comparison, St. Paul's Cathedral in London is 520 feet long. The surface area grew to 163,000 square feet. Indeed St. Peter's would remain the largest church in the world until the Our Lady of Peace of Yamoussoukro Basilica was constructed in the 1980s in the Ivory Coast, West Africa.

Maderno's nave was built upon Michelangelo's design in that the entrances to the bays are immense arches that draw the viewer's eyes up to the vaulted ceiling. He did nothing to diminish the effect of the dome. Indeed, by limiting the light in the far end of the nave, he accented the more brightly lit altar under the dome. The effect is one of looking down a tunnel of infinite length toward the center of the crossing. To each side the entrances to the chapels are dim and gloomy. Only ahead is there brightness. It is as if Maderno intended the walk up the nave to be like the journey of a troubled soul toward the light of its comforter.

While Maderno's nave was a departure from Michelangelo's plan, the casual observer would be hard put to notice the differences. The vaulted ceilings are the same height, and Maderno's columns between the bays complement the four giant piers under

This seventeenth-century painting shows St. Peter's magnificent nave shortly after its completion in 1626.

the dome. Even the slight break in the ceiling between Michelangelo's nave and Maderno's is difficult to see.

STRAIGHTENING UP

Maderno has been accused not only of departing from Michelangelo but also of failing to build his extension of the nave in a straight line from the old one. This is true. The extension is angled very slightly to the south, but Maderno had a good reason for doing so. In placing the obelisk in St. Peter's Square, Fontana had put it slightly off center of a line from the midpoint of the area under the dome down the middle of Michelangelo's nave. By angling his extension slightly, Maderno ensured that the obelisk would be exactly on a line perpendicular with the center of the exterior.

That exterior, or facade, however, has been the source of Maderno's most constant and most deserved criticism. The architect was best known for his church facades. It had been his innovative facade for the church of Santa Susanna in Rome, with its lower columns half embedded in the wall, and a balustrade, or row of posts topped by a rail, running along the roof, that had brought him to the attention of the pope. The façade of St. Peter's, however, would be a disappointment, and Maderno was probably as disappointed as anyone.

Michelangelo's design would have given the facade two rows of evenly spaced columns, much like the portico of the Pantheon.

PRAYER IN ST. PETER'S

St. Peter's has for centuries drawn people from all over the world. In more recent times, however, more have probably come as tourists than as devout pilgrims. Busloads of sightseers stream into Maderno's nave and spread throughout the basilica, many taking flash photographs.

Is St. Peter's too much of a tourist attraction, then, to fulfill its primary purpose as a church? No. Vatican officials take care to ensure that St. Peter's is first and foremost a place of worship. Services are scheduled throughout the day in the many chapels lining the nave. While they are occurring, tourists must stay out.

Confessional booths are spread throughout the nave and transepts. Each bears a sign telling not only whether or not a priest waits within to hear confessions of sin, but also which of many languages is spoken in this particular booth.

In *Vatican City,* by Orazio Petrosillo, a church official, Ennio Francia is quoted as saying it is not difficult to find a peaceful place to pray in St. Peter's. Francia wrote:

> Choose any of the chapels and you'll suddenly find yourself alone on this holy land, blessed by the blood of Peter and that of the first Christian martyrs. The building has magic, it has all the splendor that could possibly render homage to the Revelation that toppled paganism and built a new civilization on its ashes.

Maderno, however, used eight irregularly spaced columns flanked on either side by pilasters, or square columns. The spaces between the columns are filled with a hodgepodge of false windows and balconies, all overburdened with detail. The pediment, or triangular gable, appears far too small for the vast expanse, and topping it all off is an attic story. St. Peter's facade is an early example of baroque architecture with its elaborate ornamentation, and an example that shows baroque at its worst.

In Maderno's defense the way the facade turned out is not all his fault. The attic was part of Michelangelo's design and ran around the sides of the building. Maderno may have felt compelled to keep it.

This 1650 painting shows St. Peter's facade as designed by Maderno, just prior to its renovation by Gian Lorenzo Bernini.

THE BELL TOWERS

To relieve the broad, flat aspect of the facade, Maderno had designed tall bell towers on each end. He had used twin towers before in Rome and they were very well received, even though they were a departure from the usual single square tower called a campanile. The towers would have provided badly needed vertical elements for the eastern face of St. Peter's. When his workers dug the deep foundations, however, they encountered muddy soil that would have required very expensive drainage. Maderno built the bases anyway, but just before the towers were built he confessed to the pope that they would be too heavy for the foundations. Pope Paul halted construction, and two squat clock towers were eventually built on either end.

Maderno had better luck with the vestibule, or portico—the semiopen area between the facade and the five doors leading into the nave. This space, in effect the front porch of St. Peter's, is larger than many entire churches, taking in more than ten thousand two hundred square feet. The vaulted ceiling, more than sixty feet high, is filled with stucco reliefs showing episodes from the New Testament of the Bible. The floor is of highly polished, multicolored marble, and sunlight coming through the facade is reflected onto the gilded ceiling, making the entire portico luminous and bright.

Five doors lead into the nave, just as five doors led into Constantine's version of the basilica. The middle door, in fact, was in the same place in the old basilica but dates only from 1445 rather than the 300s. Like the others doors it is made of bronze and depicts religious scenes.

FILARETE'S DOOR

The central door is known simply as Filarete's Door, after the artist who cast it, but the others have names. The Door of Death, so called because it was the exit for funeral processions, is on the far left. Next is the Door of Good and Evil, with scenes of goodness on the right side and scenes torture and martyrdom on the left.

To the right of Filarete's Door is the Door of the Sacraments, the panels showing religious rites such as baptistm, marriage, holy communion, and ordination. Finally, on the far right, is the Holy Door. Most of the time this door is bricked up on the inside. But at the start of a Holy Year, which occurs every twenty-five years, the pope ceremonially strikes the bricks with a hammer whereupon they are torn down and pilgrims are allowed to enter.

THE VESTIBULE

Other works of art, dating both before and after Maderno, adorn the vestibule. There are two statues of Emperor Charlemagne on horseback: The one on the right is by Gian Lorenzo Bernini, who would have enormous influence on St. Peter's after Maderno's death. Another remarkable work, above the central door of the façade as one looks back toward the square, is a mosaic showing Jesus walking on the waters of the Lake of Galilee, motioning to Peter to come with him. It was done in the 1300s by Giotto, an exceptional artist whose work anticipated the Renaissance by seventy-five years.

A CRITIC'S OPINION

The nineteenth century French novelist Henri Beyle, who used the pen name Stendhal, had no great love for the profuse decoration of the interior of St. Peter's. He called some of the statues in Maderno's nave "ridiculous" and said that the great Altar of St. Peter in Glory in the western apse was merely pretty rather than beautiful. He also had scant respect for the Roman Catholic Church.

He could not help but be impressed by St. Peter's as a whole, however. In his journal, as quoted in *Vatican City* by Orazio Petrosillo, he wrote:

> It would be impossible not to be awed by a religion that has produced such works. Nothing in the world can compare with the interior of St. Peter's. Even after a year's residence in Rome, I would go there for hours to bask in the beauty of it.

Stendhal particularly admired Michelangelo's dome, and suggested the best way to view it:

> You must sit on a wooden bench and lean back as far as possible. That way, it will be possible to rest while contemplating the immense void that hovers above. However little one might possess of true spirituality, the imagination cannot fail to be staggered by such an experience.

Maderno endured criticism both for the nave and the facade, but he was proud of his work on the vestibule. When he was near death in 1629 he requested that he be remembered on his tombstone for only one work—the vestibule of St. Peter's.

With the completion of Maderno's nave, vestibule, and facade, the new basilica was essentially complete. On November 18, 1626 the "Temple," as it was then called, was dedicated in an elaborate ceremony by Pope Urban VIII—120 years and seven months to the day after Pope Julius II had laid the first stone.

While the basic structure of St. Peter's had been completed—the Latin cross winning out at last over the Greek—much remained to be done. The baroque era was just beginning and with it came a desire for more and more decoration. Pope Paul V and Maderno had made their contributions. Now it was time for yet another pope and artist to have their turn.

6

BERNINI'S CENTURY

Although St. Peter's Basilica was formally dedicated in 1626, much work remained to be done. Tastes had changed since Michelangelo had designed the interior. Renaissance architecture with its clean elegance had given way to the baroque with its explosion of decoration. In addition something was needed for the area in front of the basilica to relieve the dullness of Maderno's facade. The man who would spend more than fifty years working on such projects was Gian Lorenzo Bernini, an artist blessed with immense talent and the good fortune to serve under popes who appreciated it.

Pope Urban VIII had known Bernini since the days when the pope was still a cardinal and the artist was a boy learning his craft from his father, Pietro. When only nineteen years old, Bernini carved a statue of Saint Sebastian for the churchman. When Urban became pope in 1623 he was instrumental in getting Bernini a commission to remodel the Church of Santa Bibiana.

Bernini was greatly attached to Urban, but there was more to his relationship with the Vatican than his ties to one individual. He was extremely devout and regarded his work at St. Peter's to be his gift to God in addition to expressions of his art. He was also, in an era when the Roman Catholic Church faced threats from both without and within, devoted to the papacy. His works were thus intended to reflect the pope's power as Jesus' representative on Earth.

Bernini's first assignment at the Vatican was to build a *baldacchino,* or canopy, to be placed over the high altar of della Porta. He patterned his design after the canopies used to cover sacred objects as they were carried about in processions. But while these canopies were of wood and cloth, made to be carried on the shoulders of altar boys, Bernini's was bronze—an estimated seventy tons of bronze. So much bronze was needed that Pope Urban supposedly had the metal stripped from the dome and doors of the Pantheon to fill the requirement. The bronze was, indeed, removed from the ancient building during Urban's reign, but there is no hard evidence it was used on the *baldacchino.*

Deceptive Size

The amazing thing about the *baldacchino*, however, is not that it is so massive, but that it appears so small and light. Its relationship to the immense pillars that surround it and the huge dome above it is so well matched that the viewer has difficulty grasping its size—the height of a four-story building.

Bernini's baldacchino, *or canopy, over the altar is a dramatic centerpiece to the basilica, jutting four stories upward toward the dome.*

The design contributes much to the feeling of lightness and delicacy. First and foremost are the pillars at each corner—not stiff and straight, but twisted into graceful spirals, even though each one is sixty-five feet high and weighs ten tons. Bernini had legendary models to go by—the pillars that had supported the canopy over St. Peter's shrine in the earlier basilica. One of these ancient pillars supposedly had come from Solomon's Temple in Jerusalem and had been leaned on by Jesus.

Bernini, however, did much more than merely copy the old pillars. The columns are, indeed, twisted, which caused English visitors to term them "barley sugar" after a spiral candy stick traditionally made in England. The design differs in that, while the ancient columns have four alternating stages of fluting and decoration, Bernini's are in four stages with fluting on the lower one only.

THE BOY AND THE POPE

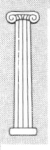

Gian Lorenzo Bernini came to the attention of the papacy at an early age. The son of a sculptor working in Rome, Bernini was first noticed by Cardinal Maffeo Barberini, later one of his greatest patrons as Pope Urban VIII. When Bernini was only ten years old, the cardinal introduced him to Pope Paul V.

According to the biography written by Bernini's son, Domenico, and quoted in *Bernini* by Charles Scribner III, the pope asked the boy to draw a head for him.

> Bernini took paper and pencil, then stopped to ask the pope: "What head does Your Holiness wish—a man or a woman, old or young, with what expression—sad, cheerful, scornful or agreeable?"
>
> "In that case," the pope said, "you know how to do everything."
>
> Bernini chose to draw a sketch of St. Paul, in whose honor the pope had chosen the name under which to reign. When he saw the drawing, the pope was so delighted that he handed Bernini a double handful of gold medals and told the cardinals surrounding them, "This child will be the Michelangelo of his age."

A detail of one of four large angels standing atop each corner of the baldacchino *shows the elaborate decoration and detail with which Bernini adorned his creation.*

Profuse Decoration

The decorated stages on the older columns consist of vines and leaves. The decoration on the newer columns is much more involved. Olive branches curl around one another profusely while naked *putti,* or cupids, frolic among them. Some frolicers reach for a swarm of bees, the symbol of Pope Urban's family, the Barberini family.

When one considers the delicacy and intricacy of the decorations, it is sometimes difficult to remember that they are executed with bronze, some of which has been gilded. The columns rest on white marble plinths, or blocks, bearing likenesses of the pope's favorite niece displaying varying emotions as she goes through pregnancy. The capitals, or tops, of the columns are decorated with more branches and bees. Between the columns hang the fringes and tassels of the canopy, on the ceiling of which is a dove sending forth rays of light.

Four large angels stand atop each corner of the square top, looking outward. Between the angels, on each side of the canopy, are *putti* holding symbols of the papacy—a Bible; a sword; the triple tiara, or crown; and the keys symbolic of St. Peter. The rest of the top consists of four graceful scrolls forming an open pyramid surmounted by a globe and cross.

The *baldacchino* is a marvel of engineering as well as of art. Bernini had to sink the foundations far below the level of the earlier basilica. Although he took care not to disturb the area immediately under the altar, where Peter is thought to have been buried, some thought Bernini was burrowing too close to sacred ground. This fear grew when both the priest in charge of the altar and his assistant died unexpectedly on the same day. When Pope Urban himself became ill, the workers refused to work further. It took the recovery of the pope and extra pay from Bernini to get them back.

BRIDGE TO THE PAST

The *baldacchino* was to be an aesthetic bridge of sorts between the new and old St. Peter's. Bernini proposed—and proceeded—to add to the decoration by hollowing out large niches in the sides of Michelangelo's giant piers that faced the altar. Statues of four saints would fill the niches, while relics of those saints would rest in loggias above them. On the sides of each loggia Bernini placed a pair of the old, twisted columns that had stood before St. Peter's shrine since the days of Constantine. Thus worshippers could see the columns that had been in the basilica more than thirteen hundred years and now looked down on newer versions of themselves.

Bernini spent seven years designing and building the *baldacchino*. Pope Urban was so pleased that he approved another project the architect had in mind—one that would be nowhere near as successful.

Like most architects of the time, Bernini looked at Maderno's disappointing facade with an eye toward what he could do to improve it. He convinced the pope that he could succeed where his predecessor had failed, constructing bell towers on either end. In fact his proposed towers would be even larger.

Bernini's Humiliation

Bernini began work in 1638. By 1641 the first two stages of the three-stage south tower were completed, and the architect placed a full-scale wooden model on top of them to show everyone how the finished product would appear. Praise was unanimous but no sooner had Bernini began to soak it up than cracks began to appear in the second stage and even in the facade itself. The Congregazione della Fabbrica hurriedly ordered that the entire tower be pulled down. Bernini was so humiliated that he shut himself away, pleading illness.

DECEIVING THE POPE

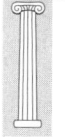

One of Gian Lorenzo Bernini's most challenging assignments at the Vatican was to create for Pope Clement IX the sound of a gushing fountain and to do it without the use of water. On the first day after his election as pope, Clement sent for Bernini, with whom he had worked closely during the papacy of Urban VIII. The new pope, it seemed, had trouble sleeping. He commissioned Bernini to renovate the Belvedere Fountain outside his private apartments, hoping that the soothing sound of rushing water would help him get a good night's sleep.

Bernini found that while he could renovate the fountain, he could not produce a water flow heavy enough to generate the sound he thought would be required. Instead he built what his son Domenico later called, as quoted in *Bernini* by Charles Scribner III, a "new and ingenious" machine. The contraption involved a rotating wheel whose spokes struck a series of paper globes, imitating the sound of rushing water.

It worked. The pope slept soundly and, when informed of how Bernini had solved the problem "could not stop saying that Bernini's genius always expressed itself in little things as well as great."

He could not put the disappointment behind him. In 1650 he proposed another solution—two free-standing towers that would not exert any strain on the facade. It might have been the best possible solution, but it was never to be. Pope Urban VIII had died and the new pope, Innocent X, had no faith in Bernini and would not approve the project.

Innocent was finally convinced of Bernini's talent, however. The pope was visiting his family palace when a friend, who was an admirer of Bernini's, managed to get him to the Piazza Navona where he saw for the first time the magnificent Fountain of the Four Rivers. Innocent was charmed with the design and commissioned Bernini to do more work at St. Peter's. The result of the pope's visit was the series of decorative reliefs on the columns of the nave and the statue of Constantine on horseback in the vestibule.

THE COURTYARD

Bernini's next great work, however, was just around the corner. Innocent died in 1655 and a new pope, Alexander VII, was elected. Alexander had been a constant friend to Bernini and on the day of his election, summoned the architect and ordered him to design a proper courtyard to the east of the basilica.

Bernini had probably been thinking about the courtyard at the same time as he was designing alternatives to the facade. His solution was entirely in keeping with his own spirituality and his belief in the power of the papacy. The design was to be two colonnades, one on each side of St. Peter's Square—two arms reaching out as if to enfold all who come seeking comfort.

The colonnades would form twin porticos, or covered walkways. Such structures had been common in ancient Roman architecture, but a curved portico was a new idea. Not only did it offer a more graceful appearance than one using right angles, but it also made the best use of the space available.

Bernini had to keep some very practical considerations in mind. First the window of the pope's private apartments had to be kept in view for a maximum number of people who gathered to receive a blessing on holy days. Second the space immediately in front of the facade was hemmed in on the north side by the Apostolic Palaces. Third the large open space already contained two features: one, Maderno's fountain, would be difficult, at best, to move; the other, the Egyptian obelisk, could be moved only at considerable expense and with a good chance it might be broken.

The two semicircular colonnades of St. Peter's Square, as designed by Bernini, were meant to symbolize outstretched and enveloping arms welcoming visitors to the basilica.

Bernini's solution was to have the arms of the colonnade angle inward slightly from the corners of the facade, so as to skirt the palace, then expand rapidly into semicircles to form a huge oval with the obelisk in the exact center. The oval was shaped so that Maderno's fountain was midway between the obelisk and the south outer edge of the colonnade. It would be complemented by a new fountain north of the obelisk.

THE COLONNADE

The colonnade consists of two double rows of forty-foot-high marble columns—284 round columns with Ionic capitals, and 88 square pilasters. The columns in each side of the oval are so precisely placed that a person standing on a point in the center of the semicircle sees only one row of columns, the others being blocked from view by the one nearest center. As a result, when one walks

A birds-eye view from the top of the southern colonnade shows the detail of various statues, each depicting a saint or pope.

through St. Peter's Square, so called even though it is an oval, there is a feeling of movement as more columns come into view and shift in their relationship to one another.

The oval is about 1,050 feet across at its widest point. The opening to the east made by the arms curving inward toward each other is about 460 feet. Bernini wanted to add a third colonnade across the eastern end, leaving two smaller openings into the square on the northeast and southeast, but the plan was too expensive for the Fabbrica to approve.

Visitors are welcomed into St. Peter's Square by much more than the arms of the colonnade. Balustrades run along the top of each structure, and on the balustrades are forty statues of saints and popes, each ten feet high, carved by Bernini's pupils. They stand along the inner edge of the colonnade, looking down on the visitors below, their backs turned to the bustle of everyday life in Rome.

It took Bernini ten years to complete the colonnade, but it was by no means his only project. At the same time he was changing the outward appearance of St. Peter's, he was similarly engaged on the inside. One of the Vatican's greatest treasures was a chair supposedly once used by Peter himself on his first visit to Rome. Actually, later investigation was to show it had been given to Pope John by Charles the Bald, grandson of Emperor Charlemagne, in 857. Such knowledge, however, has not been able to overcome the tradition that this is Peter's throne, in which he sat while preaching to the Romans.

THE *CATTEDRA*

The chair itself is made of yellow oak and acacia wood inlaid with ivory. Iron rings are attached to each leg, showing that it once could be carried in a procession. The centuries have not been kind to the relic. The wood is worm-eaten, and souvenir hunters have made off with bits and pieces over time. Pope Alexander vowed that the chair should be protected and in 1656 commissioned Bernini to make a suitable housing for it, which was called the *cattedra Petri*, or Throne of Peter.

The reverence felt for the chair was reflected in the location chosen for the monument to house it—the center of the western apse just behind the high altar where it would be in full view of anyone looking down the nave. Bernini changed his design at least twice and it is interesting to see how the work evolved. The first called for an ornate bronze throne, in which the old wooden one would be kept, to be supported by the "Four Doctors" of the church—Saints Augustine, Ambrose, Athanasius, and John Chrsysostom. Above the throne would be a sunburst in the middle of which would be an angel holding Peter's keys and the papal crown.

A subsequent version had *putti* on each side of the throne, holding the crown above it while holding keys in their other hands. Above the crown was a sunburst, but with a dove symbolic of the Holy Spirit in the middle. Large columns flanked either side, with large angels on top looking down on the dove.

In the version ultimately adopted, the four saints hold the throne but only very delicately, as if they uphold the papacy not through physical strength but through their theological support. The *putti* remain but are smaller than those depicted in the original design, dwarfed by the huge sunburst surrounded by billowing clouds, angels, and more *putti.* The most pronounced difference is the treatment of the dove. Instead of being cast in bronze it is etched in the middle of an amber and yellow glass oval, the panes of which extend from the center. The effect is highly dramatic, especially when the glass oval and dove are lit from behind through a window by the western sun.

Getting Advice

Bernini knew from the beginning that his design would need to complement that of the *baldacchino,* since the first glimpse of the monument would be framed by the giant pillars of the canopy.

> **BERNINI'S THEATRICALITY**
>
> Bernini, like numerous artists before him and since, had a streak of showmanship. Unlike Michelangelo, who was more than content to let his works speak for themselves, Bernini would sometimes present his with a flair designed to overwhelm his patrons.
>
> Early in his career he carved a bust of Cardinal Scipio Borghese. When the churchman came to view the finished work, Bernini looked sorrowful. Just as he was finishing the bust, he said, he had found a flaw in the marble. He showed the flawed work to the cardinal, who was deeply disappointed.
>
> But turning to a table nearby, Bernini plucked off a cloth covering another bust of the cardinal, this one perfect. The cardinal was overjoyed.
>
> Many years later Bernini was commissioned by Pope Innocent X to design and build a fountain in Rome's Piazza Navona. When the pope came to bless the finished work, there was no water in it. Bernini, once again longfaced, said something had gone wrong with the water supply.
>
> When Innocent turned and started to leave, however, Bernini gave a signal and water began to rush through spigots inside the statues into the basin.

With this in mind he asked the advice of an elderly painter, Andrea Sacchi, who reluctantly agreed to look at a scale model in place. When Sacchi entered the front door of the basilica, he said he needed to go no further. "This is the spot from which your work must be viewed," he told Bernini. Then he indicated the Four Doctors. "Make those statues a foot higher." Sacchi walked out without another word, and Bernini did as he recommended.[12]

The *cattedra,* formally known as the Altar of St. Peter in Glory, is also simply called Bernini's Glory. It is said to be one of the ultimate expressions of baroque art, yet is one not to everyone's taste. Protestant critics especially have condemned it for what they call an overabundance of decoration. It is perhaps best viewed, however, as an expression of devotion as well as for its artistic merits. As with Bernini's other major works at St. Peter's—the *baldacchino* and the colonnade—the *cattedra* reflected the artist's belief in the majesty of the church and the God-given authority of the pope.

Beginning and End

The *cattedra* was dedicated in a midnight ceremony in 1666, the ancient chair reverently placed in its new home. Pope Alexander died the next year. Bernini lived into his eighties but his further works at St. Peter's, though impressive, were not on the same scale as his previous ones. Over his long lifetime he had transformed the basilica. As his son, Domenico, wrote: "The *piazza* [St. Peter's Square] and the *cattedra* are, as it were, the beginning and end of that great church."[13]

The building of St. Peter's had, indeed, almost reached its end. There would be many more decorations over the centuries, and still others will come, but the church at Bernini's death in 1680 is essentially the one seen today. But while the *cattedra* may have marked an ending, the beginning still was shrouded in legend. To what extent that legend was rooted in reality would have to wait another three hundred years to be determined.

Peter's Bones

Although Bernini's work essentially completed St. Peter's, much would be built around the Vatican over the next centuries. Most of it was functional—a railroad station; a radio station; office buildings; barracks for the pope's guards; museums. The most exciting news to emerge from the Vatican, however, concerned nothing new but something very old—so old that it went back to the reason the Vatican exists.

The basilica had been built—indeed, the altar had been precisely situated—over the spot where it was believed Peter had been buried. The grave and the second-century shrine that marked it, however, had long vanished from view, incorporated into the Niche of the Pallia and the altar built for Pope Gregory I.

Tradition held firm, however, and many of Peter's successors elected to be buried as close as possible to where they believed the apostle lay. The main floor of the basilica had been raised and the lower level, the floor of which had been the floor of the earlier basilica, became known as the Vatican Grottoes. Many popes were entombed there, either above ground level in sarcophagi, monumental coffins of stone or marble, or buried just beneath the floor. Workmen digging such graves routinely discovered ancient tombs, which is logical enough since it was thought that early Christians, like the more recent popes, wanted to be buried close to Peter.

Before Pope Pius XI died in 1939, he expressed a wish to be buried as close to the site of Peter's tomb as possible. When workers began digging to the east of the Niche of the Pallia, they discovered not earlier graves but what appeared to be the top of a brick wall. They dug beside the wall and, fifteen feet down, came to a floor. Removing more dirt they found themselves in an ancient Roman mausoleum, a building housing multiple tombs. Further excavation indicated the presence of mausoleums on either side.

Working in Secrecy

When the pope was told, he assembled a team to make further investigations but instructed not to disturb the area directly under the high altar. The team was headed by Monsignor Ludwig Kaas, the chief administrator of St. Peter's, and included two archaeologists and an architect. The pope ordered them to work in the strictest secrecy. The year was now 1941, and Italy had entered World War II on the side of Adolf Hitler's Nazi Germany. The pope wanted to take no chances that the work might be discovered and interrupted by a hostile government.

The Grotto of St. Peter lies just beneath the present-day altar. The Vatican Grottoes are the remnants of the main floor of Constantine's original basilica.

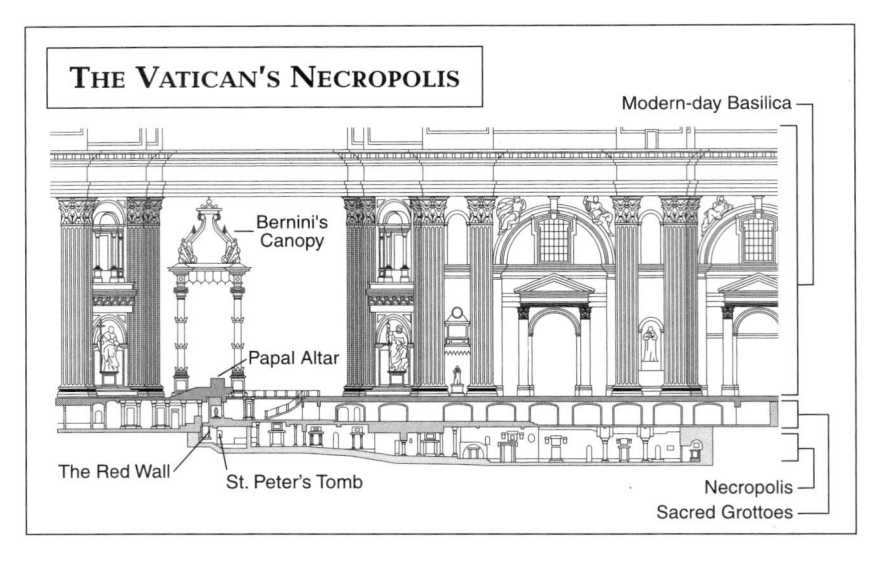

THE VATICAN'S NECROPOLIS

- Modern-day Basilica
- Bernini's Canopy
- Papal Altar
- The Red Wall
- St. Peter's Tomb
- Necropolis
- Sacred Grottoes

Above, worship went on as usual in St. Peter's. Below, usually at night, the investigators directed teams of workers. They used only pickaxes and shovels. Power tools were forbidden as being too noisy. Dirt was taken to the surface under cover of darkness and spread here and there around the Vatican Gardens. The pope wanted no mound of earth to arouse suspicion.

Gradually the team uncovered a necropolis, or city of the dead. It was an entire street, almost three hundred feet long, lined with tombs. Some were plain; others were richly decorated. Some were pagan, one was even adorned with carvings of Egyptian gods; others were obviously Christian. From the names and inscriptions on the tombs, the investigators were able to date the street from the 200s.

A Change of Mind

Pope Pius had forbidden the team to probe the area under the altar, but two things changed his mind. The first was the orientation of the street. It was clear that the tops of the mausoleums had been cut off and their interiors filled in so that the old basilica could be built in an exact location. The excavations had begun south of the altar area, and the street of tombs led uphill to the north and was pointed exactly at the altar. Clearly there was something further up the street that had caused the church to be built where it was.

The second finding that influenced Pius was an inscription found chalked on one of the tombs. Someone, perhaps one of

Constantine's workers, had written in Latin, "Peter, pray Jesus Christ for the holy men buried near your body."[14] The pope, excited by the thought that the apostle's body might actually be found, ordered the team to proceed, again under tight security.

It took them years of painstaking, shovel-by-shovel work to reach the spot directly under the altar. There they found a courtyard measuring about ten by twenty-four feet. On the western side was a red brick wall, named simply the *muro rosso,* or Red Wall, by the team. A small structure had been built into the wall. It was badly damaged but the workers could make out two niches, one above the other. A pediment, or rooflike structure, was above the

VISITING PETER'S TOMB

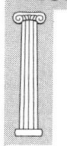

There is one part of the Vatican that, while open to visitors, is visited by very few. It is the reputed tomb of Peter that lies below the high altar, even below the Vatican Grottoes, burial place of so many of Peter's successors.

Of every thousand people who come to St. Peter's Basilica or to the Vatican museums, perhaps one takes the thirty-minute tour back through the centuries to the earliest years of Christianity. The tour is not heavily advertised, probably because only a few occur each day and each is limited to about a dozen people.

The tour begins in a room entered from the south of the basilica. After a brief introduction by the guide—each tour is conducted in a different language—the group descends a staircase to a level about twenty feet beneath the basilica floor. A sliding glass door opens briefly. The group has only twenty seconds to get through so as to let in as little outside air as possible for the protection of the artifacts within.

The door having closed behind it, the group finds itself in second-century Rome in a street of tombs, the necropolis. It winds its way west, past more insulating glass doors, to a spot directly under the altar and the dome. There, at the edge of a small courtyard, are the remnants of the small shrine to Peter erected about 170.

Anyone wanting to take the tour should plan well in advance. Reservations are almost always necessary and can be made by contacting the Uffizi Scavi, or Excavation Office, at uff.scavi@fabricsp.va.

upper niche. There were marble columns on each side of the lower niche and remains of a marble slab on top of the columns. The structure reminded the team of a place of worship so they named it the *aedicula*, or little temple.

DATING THE WALL

Had the team found the shrine of Peter the Apostle? There were tombs around the courtyard, but the investigators could not date them. However when they explored the back of the Red Wall, they found a drain that had been built the same time as the wall. The bricks carried the mark of their maker, and the team traced the mark to a factory that was making bricks between 147 and 161. This would date the Red Wall and, most likely, the *aedicula*, to the last quarter of the second century. The *aedicula*, therefore, was almost surely the "trophy" mentioned by Gaius about 200.

There were more discoveries. A marble slab in which a small hole had been cut had been placed before the *aedicula* at floor level, but at an angle slightly off perpendicular with the Red Wall. There was also a second wall, this one at a right angle to the Red Wall just north of the aedicula. It appeared to have been erected to brace the Red Wall, and its plastered surface was so covered with scratched letters and symbols that it became known as the Graffiti Wall.

Even though the team had found the shrine to Peter, there was nothing in view—an inscription, for instance—indicating that the apostle had been buried there. With the pope's blessing the investigators decided to explore under the marble slab that was level with the courtyard floor. Underneath was a cavity a bit more than two feet wide and about six and a half feet deep—very likely a grave.

COINS AND BONES

The first thing that came to light was a large pile of coins, most dating from the building of the earlier basilica to the late 500s when Pope Gregory I had paved over the site. The coins had been dropped as offerings through the hole in the marble slab by generations of pilgrims to the site.

At first the team members thought the grave held only coins, but when they looked closer they found a small pile of bones at the western end where the grave went under the Red Wall. They

HISTORICAL MAP OF THE VATICAN

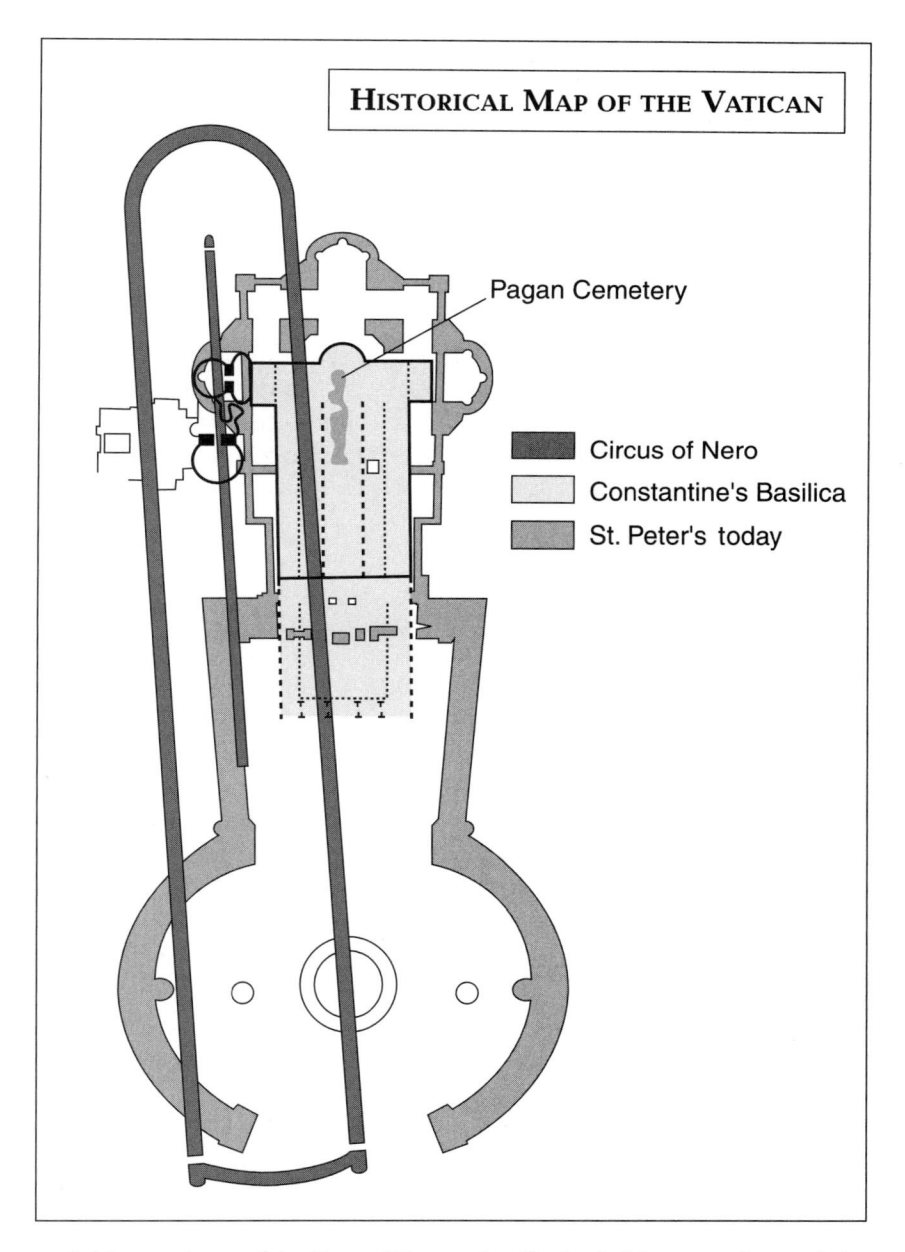

- Pagan Cemetery
- Circus of Nero
- Constantine's Basilica
- St. Peter's today

quickly sent word to Pope Pius, who that night came down into the excavation, sitting on a stool as the bones were handed up from their resting place.

Most of the bones were fragments, but some were identifiably human, such as a shoulder blade and part of a sternum. There was no skull but neither the pope nor the team expected one. A skull long believed to be that of Peter had been in another Roman basilica for a thousand years. There was no reliable way to date the bones, since the technique of radiocarbon dating had not yet been perfected. They were placed in lead boxes and given to the pope's physician for examination.

TOMBS GIVE A CLUE

Meanwhile the team began looking at other underground burials nearby. They found that two, one of a child and the other of a woman, were aligned in the same direction as the one they hoped had been Peter's. That is, they were at a slight angle to the Red Wall and thus presumably had all been dug about the same time. Luckily the woman's grave had been covered not with marble,

A GLIMPSE OF THE TOMB

It is likely that Peter's tomb remained hidden from view from 846, when the basilica was plundered by pirates, to the 1940s, when found by a team of investigators. One story, however, says that a few people got a glimpse of the saint's resting place about 1600.

When the dome had been finished, the pope at that time, Clement VIII, decided to build a new altar in place of the one erected there in the 1100s. Architect Giacomo della Porta oversaw construction.

According to the story, a large piece of masonry fell to the floor while the altar was being built, causing a crack to appear in the pavement. Looking through the crack and aided by the light of a torch, della Porta thought he could see an even older altar and a golden cross.

Pope Clement was summoned and he, too, supposedly saw what the group took to be the legendary bronze sarcophagus of Peter with the cross placed on top by St. Helena, mother of the emperor Constantine. Clement, the story goes, had no wish to disturb the holy relics, and immediately ordered the crack filled with cement.

There are two primary reasons for doubting the story. First, the plundering pirates, no respecter of relics, would hardly have left a golden cross behind. Second, the investigators in the 1940s found no such items.

but with bricks that could be traced to a workshop in operation from 69 to 79, only a few years after Peter's death.

There was one other clue. When the team studied the foundations of the Red Wall, they found that a section in the center—exactly at the point over the grave—was higher than the rest. They deduced that whoever built the Red Wall did so in order not to disturb the grave, another reason to believe the grave was much older than the wall.

The pope's doctor, meanwhile, had given his opinion. He said that the bones were those of a powerfully built man who had been sixty to seventy years old at the time of his death. This was enough proof for Pope Pius to issue a cautious statement on Christmas Eve, 1950:

> Has the tomb of St. Peter really been found? To that question the answer is beyond all doubt yes. The tomb of the Prince of the Apostles has been found. Such is the final conclusion after all the labour and study of those years. A second question, subordinate to the first, refers to the relics of St. Peter. Have they been found? At the site of the tomb remains of human bones have been discovered. However, it is impossible to prove with certainty that they belong to the apostle. This still leaves intact the historical reality of the tomb itself.[15]

ANOTHER CLUE

Even as the team's report was being published, another piece of the puzzle was found. One of the team members, archaeologist Antonio Ferrua, was visiting the site when he noticed that a fragment of the Graffiti Wall had worked loose where it abutted the Red Wall. When he examined the fragment, he found two words scratched in Greek. Some of the words were missing, but Ferrua was able to decipher them as *Petros eni,* or "Peter is within."

Just when it appeared the mystery had been solved, however, doubt was cast on the discovery. To substantiate the first opinion about the bones, they were given for further study to an expert, Venerando Correnti. Correnti studied the bones throughout the 1950s and found that they included remains from three people, an elderly woman and two younger men. In addition, some of the bones turned out to be those of farm animals.

Ancient inscriptions such as seen on this early Christian relief found in the Vatican's necropolis helped date the site and uncover the mystery of St. Peter's remains.

The initial joy of the pope and the team had now turned to disappointment, but a new phase of the investigation was about to begin. Professor Margherita Guarducci had followed the project closely, but as an expert in epigraphy, or ancient inscriptions, she was more interested in the Graffiti Wall than the bones, and secured permission to examine it.

She studied the maze of scratches and scrawls for five years and found that they were covered with Christian symbols. About twenty of them referred to Peter. But while the inscriptions may have shown that early pilgrims believed Peter was buried there, there still was no hard evidence.

THE LOCULUS

Guarducci's interest in the Graffiti Wall, however, eventually went beyond the graffiti itself. While working on the wall in 1953, she got to know Giovanni Segoni who had been a foreman on the excavation team. Guarducci was intrigued by the loculus, a space within the wall lined with marble. The team's report had said the loculus was empty, but Segoni told Guarducci a different story.

Segoni said that shortly after the Graffiti Wall was uncovered he was showing the site to Monsignor Kaas, who thought members of the team had already inspected the loculus. Kaas asked the foreman to look inside to see if anything was there. Segoni did so and discovered some bone fragments. Kaas was a priest, not a scientific investigator. He was convinced that Peter's remains, if they existed on the site, would be beneath the *aedicula* and that the bones in the loculus were just another burial. He ordered Segoni to put the bones into a box, which was then taken off for storage. Kaas neglected to report this to the team, which subsequently reported that the loculus had been empty.

At the time of her discovery, Guarducci knew Correnti was working on the bones found beneath the *aedicula*. She decided to withhold for the time being her knowledge that more bones had been discovered nearby. She changed her mind when, after Correnti had announced his initial findings, he decided to compare the *aedicula* bones with others found in the general area.

Guarducci took her concerns to the current pope, Paul VI, a close friend of her family. She told him the current location of the loculus bones and that she thought they might be much more important than first thought. The pope gave his blessing and, in 1963 and 1964, Correnti studied not only the *aedicula* and loculus bones but also the skull thought to be that of Peter.

EXPERT OPINION

Correnti found that all the loculus bones came from one person, a man about sixty-five years old in robust health. There were fragments from all parts of the body—including the skull—except the feet. If Peter had been crucified upside down, as tradition said, the Roman soldiers would probably have removed him from the cross by simply cutting off his feet. Just as significant, the supposed skull of Peter housed elsewhere in Rome did not match the bones of the loculus.

Other findings were equally compelling. Bits of earth clung to the bones. Tests showed they matched the earth in the grave below the *aedicula*. Correnti also found minute traces of purple cloth containing gold thread.

Guarducci and Correnti studied the evidence and decided that the bones of the apostle Peter had, indeed, been found. The body had originally been buried in the grave beneath the *aedicula* but moved sometime during the reign of Constantine. Perhaps, they thought, the old grave was in danger of flooding. A space was hollowed out of the Graffiti Wall and the bones, wrapped carefully in rich cloth, were placed therein.

On June 26, 1968, Pope Paul announced to the world that the remains of Peter had, indeed, been discovered. At evening on the next day, in a small private ceremony attended by Guarducci and Correnti, the pope returned the bones, protectively sealed, to the loculus.

Not All Agree

Some critics refused to accept the evidence. They contended that something grander than the loculus would have been used for the remains. They said the bones should be tested again, this time with the radiocarbon technique that could date them within 150 years of the person's death.

This fifteenth-century painting depicts the crucifixion of Saint Peter. The details of Peter's execution were scrutinized in order to help identify his bones.

This painting shows Saint Peter enthroned at the Vatican. Built upon a metaphorical rock as a symbol of devotion, the Vatican is today a complex of chapels, palaces, museums, and offices.

Pope Paul VI and his successors have refused. The evidence, they say, is conclusive enough. They refuse to once more disturb the remains of the first pope. After all, they contend, the question is in part a religious one, and there must be an element of faith involved.

The discovery of what the Roman Catholic Church believes to be the bones of Peter brought the story of the Vatican full circle. The site had progressed from a rude grave by a Roman circus, to a small shrine, to two huge basilicas, and finally to a complex of chapels, palaces, museums, and offices. In the end, however, it appears that all had been built—as Jesus had foretold—on Peter, his rock.

EPILOGUE

Just as St. Peter's stands physically in layer—from the Necropolis up through the grottoes and the basilica to the summit of the dome—so, too, the Vatican exists on different levels. On one level it is a country with its own flag, diplomatic corps, postage stamps, and even a small army. Yet it also exists on a spiritual level, a place at the center of the hearts and minds of the world's Roman Catholics. Even as it works within the world of the present, it waits patiently for the world it believes is to come.

Somewhere between seven hundred and eight hundred people actually live in the Vatican. Another four thousand are employed there, although Pope John Paul II, when once asked how many people worked in the Vatican, joked, "About half of them."[16] In addition to priests and nuns, there are museum guards and curators, maintenance workers, gardeners, librarians, choirboys, cooks, and the one hundred men of the Swiss Guard.

DWINDLING POWER

The size of the Swiss Guard underscores how the papacy has changed over time. When founded by Pope Julius II in 1509 it numbered six thousand and constituted a permanent army for this warrior pope. For centuries the papacy wielded real political power and the pope was as much an earthly king as a religious leader.

As the nations of Europe grew stronger, however, the papacy's political power dwindled. As late as 1849 the pope ruled large sections of central Italy. The area, known as the Papal States, had varied in size ever since 756, cutting the Italian peninsula in half and thus acting as a barrier to Italian unification.

The area controlled by the pope began to diminish in the 1800s, however, as the movement for Italy's unification grew stronger. By 1870 the area immediately around Rome was all that remained of the Papal States. In that year France withdrew troops it had stationed there, and on September 20, an army led by Giuseppe Garibaldi invaded Rome and declared it the capital of the kingdom of Italy.

Pope Pius IX refused to acknowledge the new state. He and his successors considered themselves prisoners in the Vatican and, once elected, never set foot outside its walls. In 1929, however, Pope Pius XI reached an agreement with what was by now the republic of Italy. The church recognized the Italian nation, and Italy paid the papacy for the loss of its lands and recognized the independence of the Vatican.

Moral Authority

Their military strength gone, the popes have become world powers in a different way. The work of the Vatican—those who live there and Roman Catholic agencies throughout the world—is now to spread Jesus of Nazareth's message and to do what it can to relieve human suffering. The pope's enemies today are not the French, Austrians, or other Italian states, but rather war, hunger, and oppression.

And all the while the Vatican waits patiently for the time when, as Christians believe, Jesus will return to earth and pass final judgment on humanity, much like what is represented in Michelangelo's fresco behind the Sistine Chapel altar. No one knows when that day will come, but waiting is one of the things the Vatican does best. The tradition of the Holy Roman Emperor receiving his crown from the hands of the pope, begun with Emperor Charlemagne in 800, died out in 1530. Indeed there has been no Holy Roman Empire for more than two hundred years. And yet deep within the Vatican, in the pope's private treasure, hangs a richly decorated cloak. It is reserved for the Holy Roman Emperor, if ever there should again be one.

Notes

Chapter 1: The Emperors' Hill
1. Quoted in Bart McDowell, *Inside the Vatican*. Washington, D.C.: National Geographic Book Division, 1991, p. 29.
2. Quoted in James Lees-Milne, *St. Peter's*. Boston: Little, Brown, 1966, p. 72.

Chapter 2: The Pope's Palace
3. Quoted in Orazio Petrosillo, *Vatican City*. Vatican City: Ufficio Vendita Pubblicazioni e Reproduzioni dei Musei Vaticani, 2000, p. 39.
4. Quoted in Nicolò Suffi, *St. Peter's: Guide to the Square and the Basilica*. Vatican City: Libreria Editrice Vaticana, 1998, p. 93.
5. Quoted in Fabrizio Mancinelli, *The Sistine Chapel*. Vatican City: Ufficio Vendita Pubblicazioni e Reproduzioni dei Musei Vaticani, 2000, p. 80.
6. Quoted in Mancinelli, *The Sistine Chapel*, p. 50.

Chapter 3: The Greek Cross
7. Quoted in Lees-Milne, *St. Peter's*, p. 124.
8. Quoted in *Jubilee 2000: The 7 Basilicas of Rome*. Narni, Casa Editrice Plurigraf, 2000, p. 35.
9. Quoted in Lees-Milne, *St. Peter's*, p. 167.
10. Quoted in Lees-Milne, *St. Peter's*, p. 184.
11. Michelangelo Buonarroti, *Michelangelo: A Self-Portrait*. Robert J. Clements, ed., New York: New York University Press, 1968, p. 121.

Chapter 6: Bernini's Century
12. Quoted in Lees-Milne, *St. Peter's*, p. 279.
13. Quoted in Lees-Milne, *St. Peter's*, p. 281.

Chapter 7: Peter's Bones
14. Quoted in John Curran, "The Bones of St. Peter?," *Classics Ireland*. Dublin, Ireland: University College, 1996.
15. Quoted in Curran, "The Bones of St. Peter?," *Clasics Ireland*.

Epilogue
16. Quoted in McDowell, *Inside the Vatican*, p. 16.

For Further Reading

Books

Vittorio Giudici, *The Sistine Chapel,* trans. Anthony Brierley. New York: Peter Bedrick, 2000. Tells the story not only of the works of art in the chapel, but also those of the men who painted them and the popes who commissioned them.

William W. Lace, *The Importance of Michelangelo.* San Diego, CA: Lucent Books, 1993. Tells the story of the artist's life and works with special attention to the influence he had on future artists and architects.

Julian Morgan, *Constantine: Ruler of Christian Rome.* New York: Rosen, 2003. Nicely written and illustrated account of how one man raised Christianity from a despised minority to the official religion of the mighty Roman Empire.

Renee C. Rebman, *The Sistine Chapel.* San Diego, CA: Lucent, 2000. The story of how a chapel became a canvas on which some of the greatest artists in European history displayed their talents.

Diane Stanley, *Michelangelo.* New York: HarperCollins Juvenile Books, 2000. Lively and beautifully illustrated account of the life and works of the great Renaissance artist.

Websites

Catholic Encyclopedia (http://www.newadvent.org/cathen). Comprehensive site on which can be found, among many other listings, biographical sketches of every pope and every Vatican architect.

Michelangelo Buonarroti (www.michelangelo.com/buonarroti.html). Superb website that features biographical information, photographs, reference lists, and even a Renaissance music accompaniment.

History of Constantine the Great (www.shsu.edu/~eng-wpf/con-hist.html). Divided into sections including history and biography, art and architecture, paintings, and others.

Works Consulted

Books

Antonio Alberti-Poja, *The House of Peter.* Trans. Edoardo Canali. Gerrard's Cross, England: Van Duren, 1987. More a history of the papacy than of the Vatican, this highly readable book nevertheless has good chapters on art and architecture.

Michelangelo Buonarroti, *Michelangelo: A Self-Portrait.* Ed. Robert J. Clements. New York: New York University Press, 1968. Collection of the most revealing of Michelangelo's many letters, poems, and sayings arranged by topic. Gives an excellent view of the artist through his own words.

Jérôme Carcopino, *The Vatican.* London: Thames and Hudson, 1964. Although the text is somewhat dated, this large, beautiful book is filled with photographs, many in color. The photos of the Sistine Chapel ceiling before restoration are interesting to compare with more recent photos.

Robert Coughlan, *The World of Michelangelo, 1475–1564.* New York: Time-Life Books, 1966. Excellent overall account of the artist and his work. Especially helpful in describing how the political events of the time affected Michelangelo.

Jubilee 2000: The 7 Basilicas of Rome. Narni, Italy: Casa Editrice Plurigraf, 2000. Special guidebook published for the Jubilee Year. Good, basic information, not only on St. Peter's, but also on St. John Lateran and five other Roman basilicas.

James Lees-Milne, *St. Peter's.* Boston: Little, Brown, 1966. Written by a well-known English architectural historian, this is one of the most comprehensive and readable accounts available of the development of St. Peter's Basilica.

Fabrizio Mancinelli, *The Sistine Chapel.* Vatican City: Ufficio Vendita Pubblicazioni e Reproduzioni dei Musei Vaticani, 2000. Official Vatican guidebook to the Sistine Chapel provides comprehensive examination, not only of the ceiling and the *Last Judgment,* but also the many other treasures sometimes overlooked.

Bart McDowell, *Inside the Vatican.* Washington, DC: National Geographic Book Division, 1991. The text by McDowell is completely overshadowed by the dozens of photographs, many of them very candid pictures of the everyday lives of the pope and those around him, taken by James L. Stanfield over more than a year at the Vatican.

Aubrey Menan, *Upon This Rock.* New York: Saturday Review Press, 1972. Entertaining, chatty, and somewhat opinionated description of the various stages of construction of St. Peter's Basilica.

Francesco Papafava, *Guide to the Vatican Museums and City.* Vatican City: Gestioni Vendita Pubblicazioni Musei Vaticani, 1986. For the most part, this is a guide to the works in the Vatican museums, but there is also very good information on the basilica, the Apostolic Palace, and the necropolis.

Orazio Petrosillo, *Vatican City.* Vatican City: Ufficio Vendita Pubblicazioni e Reproduzioni dei Musei Vaticani, 2000. Informative, lavishly illustrated description published by the official publications office of Vatican City.

Charles Scribner III, *Bernini.* New York: Harry N. Abrams, 1991. Comprehensive examination of Bernini's works. Much of the book consists of full-page color photographs of major works, each accompanied by a page of descriptive text.

Nicolò Suffi, *St. Peter's: Guide to the Square and the Basilica,* trans. Kate Marcelin-Rice. Vatican City: Libreria Editrice Vaticana, 1998. Highly detailed description of the chapels, decorations, and works of art found in both St. Peter's Basilica and outside in St. Peter's Square.

Jocelyn Toynbee and John Ward Perkins, *The Shrine of St. Peter and the Vatican Excavations.* New York: Pantheon, 1957. Extremely detailed but highly technical description of the necropolis found beneath St. Peter's Basilica in the 1940s. For the serious student of anthropology or archaeology.

Giorgio Vasari, *The Lives of the Painters, Sculptors, and Architects.* Trans. A.B. Hinds. London: J.M. Dent and Sons, 1973. Short biographies of all major and minor figures of Italian Renaissance art. The section on Michelangelo is the best primary source for biographical details.

Robert Wallace, *The World of Bernini, 1598–1680.* New York: Time-Life Books, 1970. Highly informative account of the life and works of Gian Lorenzo Bernini, all told in the context of the times in which he lived. Contains ample photographs and illustrations.

Internet Source

John Curran, "The Bones of St. Peter?," *Classics Ireland*, Vol. 3, 1996. University College Dublin, Ireland. http://www.ucd.ie/classics/96/Curran96.html.

Index

abbots, 81
Ackerman, J.S., 48
aedicula, 106, 111
Africa, 64
Agrippina, 64
aisles, 22, 38
Alberti, Leon Battista, 38
alms, 40
altar, 21, 42, 61
Alexander VI, 29, 39
Alexander VII, 96, 99, 101
amphitheater, 14, 16
Angelico Fra, 28
Apostolic Palace, 25, 27, 29, 31, 34, 37
apse, 20, 21, 22, 42
archaeologists, 103
archbishops, 23
architects, 42, 50, 54, 58, 62, 81
architecture, 10, 48, 86, 90, 96
artists, 27, 29, 30, 33, 34, 82, 88
arts, work of, 28, 42, 54, 90
atrium, 36, 38
Avignon (France), 23

Babylonian Captivity, 24, 38
baldacchino, 12, 90–94, 100, 101
balustrades, 85, 98
baptistery, 83
Barberini, Maffeo, 92
baroque art, 81, 89, 90, 101
Battle of Milvian Bridge, 19
bell towers, 87, 95
Belvedere Fountain, 95
Belvedere Villa, 35
Belvedere, Court of, 28, 36, 39

Bernini, Domenico, 92, 95
Bernini, Gian Lorenzo, 12, 92, 94, 97
 death of, 101
 designs *baldacchino*, 90
 designs *cattedra*, 100
 is humilated, 95
 works of art by, 88
Bernini (Scribner), 92, 95
Beyle, Henri, 88
Bible, 16, 29, 87
bishops, 21, 81
Bologna (Italy), 47
bones, 106, 108, 109, 110, 111, 112
Bordighera, 59–60
Borgia Apartments, 29, 39
Borgia Tower, 29, 39
Bramante, Donato, 34–35, 61, 62
 designs Greek cross, 41
 demolition of basilica and, 42, 43
Britain, 14, 17
bronze, 90, 94
Brunelleschi, Filippo, 53, 54
bullfights, 36
Buonarroti, Michelangelo. *See* Michelangelo
Byzantium. *See* Constantinople

Caligula, 14, 58
Cambio, Arnolfo di, 43
canopy. *See baldacchino*
cardinals, 62, 81, 82
Castle of San Angelo, 27
cattedra Petri, 21, 99–100, 101
carvings, 104
cemetery, 19, 24

Cesena, Biagio da, 35
chancel, 21, 22
chapels, 28, 37, 82
chariot races, 14
Charlemagne, 25, 88, 99, 115
Charles V (German emperor), 45
Charles the Bald, 99
Christian religion, 14, 61, 115
  cross and, 41, 44
  persecution and, 16–17
  Roman Empire and, 18
Church of Bibiana, 90
Church of Santa Susanna (Rome), 85
Church of St. Paul, 55
circus, 14, 19, 58, 113
Circus of Maximus, 16
Claudius, 15
Clement VII, 45
Clement VIII, 61, 62
Clement IX, 95
codices, 28
coffin. *See* sarcophagi
coins, 106
College of Cardinals, 30
colonnades, 96, 97–99, 101
columns, 22, 39, 64, 94
Committee for the Building of St. Peter's. *See* Fabbrica
confession booths, 85
congregation, 21
Congregazione della Fabbrica di San Pietro. See Fabbrica.
consecration, 23
Constantine, 17–20, 23, 38, 94, 108
Constantinople, 23
Correnti, Venerando, 109, 111, 112
Coughlan, Robert, 35, 54

Council of Nicea, 18
Court of Pine Cone, 37
Court of Saint Damascus, 37
courtyard, 19, 22, 24, 36–37, 96–97
cross, 17, 18
  see also Greek cross; Latin cross
crowns, 25, 42, 115
crucifixion, 14, 17
Cybele (goddess), 13

della Porta, Giacomo, 50, 54, 55, 61, 62, 108
domes, 41, 42, 48, 51, 56,
  clearer view of, 52
  decoration of, 57
  design changes of, 52–55
  size of, 53–54
doors, 87, 88
dove symbols, 99, 100
Duomo, 53, 54

Edict of Milan, 18–19
Edict of Toleration. *See* Edict of Milan
Egyptian gods, 104
England, 45, 92
epigraphy, 110
Europe, 23, 29, 40, 62, 114
Excavation Office, 105
excavations, 102–104, 111

Fabbrica, 45, 57, 62, 64, 95, 98
facades, 85, 86, 89, 90, 96, 97
fasting, 40
Feast of Exaltation of the Cross, 59
Ferrua, Antonio, 109
Filaretes Door, 87
fire, 16

Florence (Italy), 31, 38
Fontana, Domenico, 28, 37, 58, 59, 84
Fountain of Four Rivers, 96
fountains, 95, 96, 97, 100
France, 25, 26, 114
Francia, Ennio, 85
fresco, 31, 33, 34, 42, 48, 115

Gaius, 17, 106, 119
Galilee, 15
Garibaldi, Giuseppe, 114
Germany, 45
Giocando, Fra, 43
Giotto, 88
God, 18, 22, 33, 57, 90
Graffiti Wall, 106, 109, 110, 112
Great Niche, 36
Great Western Schism, 27, 38
Greece, 22
Greek cross, 42, 47, 62, 81
  designed by Bramante, 41
  dimensions of, 48
  transformed to Latin cross, 44–45
Gregory I, 22, 23, 106
Gregory III, 43
Gregory VII, 23
Gregory XI, 25
Gregory XIII, 37, 50
Guarducci, Margherita, 110, 111, 112

Hadrian, 52, 83
Hare, Augustus, 52
Henry IV, 23
high altar, 12, 41, 61, 90, 103
Hill of Prophecy, 13
historians, 20, 27, 53, 118
Hitler, Adolf, 103

Holy Roman Empire, 23, 25
Holy Spirit, 99
Holy Year, 87

incunabula, 28
Innocent VIII, 29, 39
Innocent X, 96, 100
invasions, 23, 45
Italy, 10, 27, 29, 45, 83, 103, 114
Ivory Coast, 83

Jerusalem, 22, 28, 92
Jesus Christ, 40, 41, 43, 55
  crucifixion of, 14
  disciples and, 12, 16
  judgment and, 115
  prophecy about Peter and, 113
  work of art about, 30, 83, 88
jousting, 36
Julius II, 37, 38, 47, 49, 114
  election of, 29
  death of, 42
  Michelangelo and, 31–32, 34
  raised funds, 39, 40
Jupiter (Roman god), 43

Kaas, Ludwig, 103, 111

lantern, 55, 56, 57, 58
Last Jugdment, The (Michelangelo), 34, 35, 46
Lateran Palace, 25
Latin cross, 43, 47, 81, 82, 89
Lees-Milne, James, 19
Leo I, 43, 44
Leo IV, 23, 27
Leo X, 43
Licinius, 19
Ligorio, Pirro, 50

Lives of Painters, Sculptors, and Architects (Vasari), 47
loggia (galleries), 35, 37, 94
London, 83
Luther, Martin, 40

Maderno, Carlo
  appointed as architect, 62,
  designed Latin cross, 81–82
  criticism of, 83, 84–85, 86, 89
  facade and, 87, 89, 90
mantle, 22, 23
marble, 22, 30
Mary (mother of Jesus), 30, 82, 83
mass, 12, 58
mausoleums, 19, 102, 104
Maxentius, 17–18
Medici family, 38
medieval, 43
Messiah. *See* Jesus Christ
Michelangelo, 12, 38, 39, 50, 55
  as architect, 46
  art works and paintings of, 30-31, 33, 35, 48, 115
  death of, 49
  designs Greek cross, 47, 48,
  Pietà and, 82, 83,
Minerva (goddess), 21
miracles, 22
Mons Vaticanus. See Hill of Prophecy
monuments, 63, 83
mosaics, 42, 56, 88
museums, 102
Mussolini, Benito, 52

nave, 20, 81, 83–84, 87
necropolis, 19, 104, 105, 114
Nero, 14, 16, 19

New World, 40
Niche of the Pallia, 23, 61, 102
Nicholas III, 25, 27, 28
Nicholas V, 27, 28, 37, 38, 39
Ninety-Five Theses (Luther), 40
nuns, 45, 114

obelisk, 58, 59, 61, 84, 96, 97
Old Testament, 32
Ostia, 14
Our Lady of Peace of Yamoussoukro Basilica, 83

paganism, 61
painters, 28, 29, 44, 101
paintings, 37
palaces, 25, 35–37
Palestine, 14, 15
pallia. See mantle
Palm Sunday, 60, 83
Pantheon, 41, 52, 53, 54, 85, 90
papacy, 38
  moved to France, 23
  political authority and, 96, 114
  return of, to Rome, 25
  spiritual powers of, 15,
  symbols of, 94
papal robes, 31
Pappagallo, 26, 27
Pappagallo Court, 28
Paul III, 33–34, 35, 45, 47
Paul V, 81, 89, 92
Paul VI, 111, 113
Peruzzi, Baldassare, 44–45
Peter, 12, 14, 88
  bones of, 111, 112, 113
  character and, 16
  crucifixion of, 17

grave of, 20, 61, 110
shrine of, 22, 23
statue of, 43
tomb of, 19, 39, 61, 105
Petrosillo, Orazio, 85, 88
Philip IV (king of France), 23
Piazza Navona, 100
piers, 42, 44, 45
Pietà (Michelangelo), 82, 83
pilgrims, 22, 85, 88, 110
pillars, 91, 92
Pinturicchio (artist), 29
pirates, 23, 105
plaza. *See* St. Peter's Square
popes, 63
  election of, 31
porticos, 10, 81
prayers, 31, 40
priests, 22, 45, 62
Protestant Reformation, 40, 45

radiocarbon dating, 108, 112
Raphael, 34, 35, 43, 44
Red Wall, 105, 109
relics
  relocation of, 63–64
  sacredness of, 99, 108
  of saints, 63, 94
religious rites, 87
Renaissance, 29
  architectural designs of, 43, 48, 53, 54, 81, 88
  artists of, 82
Roman Catholic Church, 10, 90
  beliefs, 15, 56, 113
  split in, 40
Roman Catholics, 114, 115
Roman Empire, 14
Rome, 10, 12, 23, 55, 58, 61
  as capital of Italy, 114

invasion of, 45
papacy in, 25
Rossellino, Bernardo, 38, 64

Sacchi, Andrea, 101
saints, 98
Sampietrini, 57
Sangallesca, 45, 47, 49
Sangallo, Antonio da, 43, 45–47
Sangallo, Giuliano da, 38, 43
Sanzio, Rafaello. *See* Raphael
Saracens, 23
sarcophagi, 83, 102
Satan, 16
School of Athens (Raphael), 34
Scipio, Borghese, 100
Scribner, Charles, III, 92, 95
scripture, 28
sculptor, 31, 43, 48, 83
Segoni, Giovanni, 111
Sistine Chapel, 28, 29, 31–34, 38, 39
Sixtus IV, 38
Sixtus V, 54–55, 58, 60
  built palace, 37
  commissioned library, 28, raised funds, 50–52
  Sistine chapel and, 30
  split courtyard of, 36
  as uncle of Julius II, 64
slaves, 15
Solomon's Temple, 22, 28, 92
spectators, 58
statuary, 42
statues, 26, 55, 96, 98
  of angels, 94
  Charlemagne and, 88
  evangelists and, 56
  of mythical birds, 26

of Peter, 43
Pietà as, 30, 82, 83
Stanze, 34
Stendhal. *See* Beyle, Henri
St. Helena, 108
St. John Lateran, 19, 25
St. Paul's Cathedral (London), 83
St. Peter's (Lees-Milne), 19, 52
St. Peter's Basilica, 53, 54, 57
  abandoned, 23–24
  dedication of, 90, 101
  demolition of, 42–43, 45, 61, 62–64, 83
  designs of, 20–23
  deterioration of, 24
  funds and, 49, 52, 62
  location of, 10, 19–20
  rebuilding of, 38-39
  as spiritual haven, 114
  as tourist attraction, 12, 83, 85
St. Peter's Square, 10, 31, 37, 52, 58, 98
Swiss Guard, 114

Tacitus, 17
Tiber River, 10, 14, 27, 35, 52
tombs, 19, 63, 64, 83, 102, 104
tourists, 28, 33, 83, 85
Tower of Nicholas V, 27, 37
treasury, 27, 40, 52
Turkey, 31

Twelve Apostles, 12, 15, 20

Urban VIII, 89, 90, 92, 94, 95, 96

Vasari, Gregorio, 33, 34, 47, 82
Vatican, 36, 115
  archivist and, 63
  gardens of, 104
  grottoes of, 102, 105
  library of, 27, 28
  museums of, 25, 28, 105
Vatican City (Petrosillo), 85, 88
Vatican Hill, 13, 16, 20, 29
Venice, 46
vestibule, 87, 88, 89, 96
Via della Conciliazione, 10, 52
Via di Porta Angelica, 10
Vignola, Jacopo, 50
vision, 18
Volterra, Daniele da, 35

West Africa, 83
Wittenburg, 40
World of Michelangelo, The (Coughlan), 35, 54
World War II, 103
worship, 31, 86
worshippers, 20, 22, 94

Zabagila, 57

Picture Credits

Cover Images: © Timothy McCarthy/Art Resource, NY, Planet Art, © Vittoriano Rastelli/CORBIS
© Alinari/Art Resource, NY, 32, 36
© Archivo Iconografico, S.A./CORBIS, 44, 84
© Bridgeman Art Library, 41
© Historical Picture Archive/CORBIS, 59
© William W. Lace, 69, 81
© Erich Lessing/Art Resource, NY, 15, 53, 86
© Araldo de Luca/CORBIS, 74
© Mary Evans Picture Library, 14
© John and Lisa Merrill/CORBIS, 67
© Sergio Pitamitz/CORBIS, 68
© Reunion des Musees Nationaux/Art Resource, NY, 39, 113
© Reuters NewMedia Inc./CORBIS, 98
© Royalty-Free/CORBIS, 76
© Saskia Ltd./Art Resource, NY, 91, 93
© Scala/Art Resource, NY, 11, 18, 21, 26, 33, 46, 51, 53, 64, 65, 70, 71, 72, 73, 75, 77, 78, 79, 80, 97, 103, 110, 112
© Ted Spiegel/CORBIS, 82
© David Turnley/CORBIS, 68
© Ruggero Vanni/CORBIS, 60
Steve Zmina, 13, 30, 48, 56, 63, 104, 107

About the Author

William W. Lace is a native of Fort Worth, Texas. He holds a bachelor's degree from Texas Christian University, a master's degree from East Texas State University, and a doctorate from the University of North Texas. After writing for newspapers in Baytown, Texas, and Fort Worth, he joined the University of Texas at Arlington, eventually becoming director of the News Service. He is now executive assistant to the chancellor at Tarrant County College in Fort Worth. He has written more than twenty books for Lucent, one of which—*The Death Camps* in the Holocaust Library series—was selected by the New York Public Library for its 1999 Recommended Teenage Reading List. He and his wife Laura, a retired school librarian, live in Arlington, Texas, and have two grown children.

BETHLEHEM PUBLIC LIBRARY

3 8113 10088 4300

am W.

JAN - 3 2005

DATE			

BETHLEHEM PUBLIC LIBRARY
451 DELAWARE AVENUE
DELMAR, NY 12054 (518)439−9314
WWW.BETHLEHEMPUBLICLIBRARY.ORG

BAKER & TAYLOR